The Art of Selling Movies

JOHN   ETHEL   LIONEL

BARRYMORE

RASPUTIN and the EMPRESS

UNITED

FLOOR FOR RENT
ONE FLIGHT UP — Suitable for BEAUTY PARLOR or OFFICES
Apply WALTER READE IN THIS 1531 BROADWAY
TEL. CHICKERING 4-5800

CALUMET

Doughnuts and Coffee 15¢

MAYFLOWER DOUGHNUTS

ASTOR THEATRE

JOHN • ETHEL & LIONEL BARRYMORE
RASPUTIN AND THE EMPRESS

The Art of Selling Movies

John McElwee

GoodKnight Books
Pittsburgh, Pennsylvania

GoodKnight Books

©2017 by John McElwee

All rights reserved. No part of this book may be reproduced or transmitted in any form or by any means, electronic or mechanical, including photocopying, or by an information storage and retrieval system without permission in writing from the publisher.

Published by GoodKnight Books, an imprint of Paladin Communications
Pittsburgh, Pennsylvania

Printed in the United States of America

First Edition

Library of Congress Control Number: 2016954734

ISBN: 978-0-9962740-4-3

To all fans, collectors, and movie lovers from the very beginning who saved theatre ads from newspapers. Whether in scrapbooks or file folders, or loose among torn tickets and diary entries, these mementos speak for joy of show-going during a vanished era when art plus enterprise made film promoting a daily and closely followed ritual in every corner of the United States. Ones who did the gathering are mostly gone, left little record even of who they were, but what they'd preserve and cherish then will hopefully be as meaningful for us now.

Contents

The Art of Selling Movies

Preface

*Imagine you've been hired to manage a theatre. Or maybe you bought one, and now comes the job of running it. As with any business, there's a learning process, details anyone of reasonable intelligence can learn and eventually apply. Here's the rub: You're in show **business**, a decidedly creative enterprise. You must appeal to sensibilities more complicated than neighbor merchants with their bread loaves and lawn mowers.*

Advertising movie after movie calls for nonstop engagement of readers' eyes plus penetration of minds, your platform a sliver of newspaper space. Folks won't attend just because your theatre is open and showing films. Plenty of venues, some on the same block, are doing as much. You have to sell your show but also take attendance away from other shows. Customers can't pay into two theatres at once, won't visit both on a same evening (but for far-gone fans), so theirs is to choose, and yours is to make sure they choose you.

No stress really, for it is only your livelihood at stake.

During the Classic Era (silents to mid-1960s) men and women with no aptitude for art had to become artists, wizards with words, master persuaders. Ad folk for other product rose to similar challenge, but they pitched tangible merchandise. Theatre operators sold a couple hours' amusement, but gave customers nothing to carry home other than memories each hoped would be pleasant. Happy times were promised daily amidst heated competition on the Amusement Page.

Maybe they thought starting out that to run a theatre was simple as tearing tickets and popping corn. Being a wiz at projection or on-site displays went but so far, for sales were mostly closed in homes, on streetcars, at the barber shop or beauty salon—wherever folks read newspapers. Theatre managers had to master print ads or hire someone who could. There was no third way, short of lost attendance and eventually shuttered doors.

This is not necessarily a "movie book." Hundreds of movies are represented, but I'm less for talking about them than about the skill, sometimes genius, of pulling paid admissions through a showman's entrance door. As exhibitor and MGM co-founder Marcus Loew famously said, "We sell tickets to theatres, not movies." Loew understood it was entirety of the show that mattered, not just the feature, or even a feature with shorts. His operation and ones like it sold show-going as an event in itself, one that began not in the auditorium, the lobby, or even the decorated front, but with ads to promise attendees a happy night out.

Let's give great directors and iconic stars a rest, so that faceless folk who made them look good can take a bow. I've wondered if industry players clipped and saved ads for films they'd made, or even saw such ads. It wouldn't have been easy keeping up with so

Starlight Drive-In

My kind of town to grow up in and typical of ads I clipped from our local newspaper during the mid-'60s.

many that were generated across a nation, make that a world, exposed to American films. And yet here's where people inside the picture industry could learn much about how their work was presented to a mass public. Much truth about the business was unique to theatre ads, those furthest from urban centers often the most illuminating.

Ads were crucial to success for not only a film they'd promote, but for future engagements of that same film. It often was a matter of creating the perception of a hit, being noticed by surrounding exhibitors who'd then seek the allegedly proven product for their own house. Effective ads were seen by fans as well, many spreading word not only among neighbors but to neighboring towns.

It had not always been so. Newspaper ads took years to penetrate a selling landscape. Infancy saw movies coming and going too quick to benefit from print promotion. Add to that fact of few films lasting over a single reel or two. This was the case from introduction of cinema through a decade and a half that followed, an era where folks got in for a nickel and it hardly mattered what was on-screen, so long as it briefly amused. Storefront theatres changing programs daily weren't tempted to spend for newspaper advertising. That would come with larger auditoriums, an emerging star system, and longer movies they'd dub "features." Finish of a first decade of the 1900s saw motion pictures begin transition from nickelodeons to grandeur of urban palaces and even small towns seating patronage by the hundreds in comparative luxury. Newspapers had ignored the emerging art for simple reason that showmen weren't so far buying ad space, so why take movies seriously?

Film had to organize along industrial lines to truly make the grade. An audience captured nationwide was the essential, not mere locals pursuing a fad. Dollars spent for print ads would grease path toward making movies "news." Nickelodeons had hooked enough of a public to demand media coverage for films and people who made them. Calendars turning from 1911 to 1912 saw rapid rise of interest in movie matters. Till then, it

Arabesque

Pardon excess of scotch tape used for adding this Charlotte, North Carolina, ad from 1966 to my scrapbook, but how did I know it would be needed for this book a half century later?

A 1956 Los Angeles Amusement Page shows crowded landscape that was mid-century theater promoting. Note the tiny ad for a *Citizen Kane* reissue in the upper center-right.

Robin Hood Drive-In

Five features and three Road Runners sounds exhausting, though we may assume patrons to Winston-Salem's Robin Hood Drive-In in 1958 didn't find it so.

was trade publications spreading the word, but who among wider public sought these out? Now would come full-page reportage in many Sunday papers, daily mention elsewhere per reader demand, as films gained a mass following.

Spirit of competition and a swelling fan base made theatres tout wares in ever-larger ads. Increased popularity of stars made their images essential to print displays, with title, time, date, and other policy commanding space beyond single columns toward quarter, half, even whole newspaper pages. By the mid-teens, theatre ads approached a volume to compete with mainstream promotion of goods and services to daily readership.

No book, even in multi-volumes, could cover all of ads that showmen generated over three quarters of a century that represented newspaper selling during a Classic Era. There were so many hundreds of thousands of individual ads, most regrettably gone via fragile and disposable paper they were printed on. *The Art Of Selling Movies* can but sample from representative survivors of an epoch gone even before dailies themselves saw eclipse by digital spread of news.

Childhood movie itch began for me with newspaper advertising. I'd skip comic pages to see what theatres were playing. When hour-away Winston-Salem, North Carolina, got a newest James Bond or Elvis, I'd ask our downtown house when we'd have them. (Answer: "When snow flies . . ." or "When leaves fall . . ." Anyway, not for weeks, if not months.)

From age five I cut ads from newspapers. There was a scrapbook, in fact several, by the finish of kindergarten. Neighbors with newspaper subscriptions other than my family's own saw me rummage often through their *Charlotte Observer* or *Greensboro Daily Record.* I had an imaginary theatre called the "Parkland" for which I drew ads on school notebook paper. The Parkland ran all the pictures I wanted to see, even if only in my dreams.

This book represents partial bounty of what I accumulated over decades gathering ads. They're mostly yellowed, some with bled-through print or other distress. Photoshop can help, in fact work miracles at times, but nothing will make survivors look fresh as they did in morning editions just printed. Frankly, I wouldn't have them any other way. Tanned pages with an occasional rip hath charm for this ad collector, and I hope for readers as well.

I was able to ID most towns these promotions represent but not all, for a lot came my way in albums kept by long-ago show folk or fans who clipped from newspapers same as me but didn't note which ones. I cherish such tracks off advertising's desert filled by sands of time. Maybe someone reading, perhaps you, will recognize a theatre I did not and identify its location. If so, do drop a note c/o Greenbriar Picture Shows, online address for this author since 2005 and home to musings on shows and showmanship, classic and otherwise.

Thanks to Howard Mandelbaum at Photofest for theatre front images on pages 14 and 15, and to Bruce Hershenson for marquee photos on pages ii, x, xvi, 148, 216, and 262. And thanks to Karl Thiede for review of the manuscript and helpful suggestions. A big thank you goes to Sharon Berk for her design of the book and to Valerie Sloan for fantastic work in restoring these ads that were close to being lost forever.

'THE SPIDER' IS BIGGER THAN THE PLAYHOUSE!

THE SPIDER
It Must Eat You
To Live!

'The Spider' starts Thurs., at the Playhouse
Also Showing—'THE BRAIN EATERS'—A Science Fiction Thriller!

The Spider

The Spider makes a meal of the Playhouse Theatre's marquee! Could Statesville, North Carolina, populace stand such onslaught of terror?

Introduction:
Fine Art, Folk Art, or No Art at All

'd like everyone reading this book to come away proclaiming movie ads a great lost art. That'll be a high hill to climb, thanks to base commercial purpose for which theatre advertising, at least in newspapers, was created. Aesthetics had nothing to do with it and still doesn't for what little is left of film promotion in dailies; for that matter, what future is left for dailies themselves?

Today, there are a multitude of ways to announce what's playing at theatres. Websites, Facebook, any and all means of access by smartphone, along with previewing and direct appeal from filmmakers off Internet clouds. All this evolved since learning a show's place and time meant checking a newspaper or walking by a theatre front to read the marquee. These required purchase of a newspaper or travel by foot or vehicle to whatever venue was the object of curiosity. Either way took money or time. It was for theatre operators to make that effort pleasant as possible. A richly decorated entrance could entice passersby to a show, then or later when they had hours to spare. Otherwise, it was necessary to sell them in print, in black and white and shades between.

Theatre ads during the Classic Era, which I propose to be from movie beginnings to approximately the mid-1960s, were documents of selling as practiced by local showmen, the grass roots of promotion. These managers were guided by instinct and individual initiative when it came to marketing of films shown. No one in their city or community, certainly no one outside it, understood so well what it took to draw a paying crowd. Is it folly to refer to such showmen as folk artists? Based on results so many got with ads, all done on short schedule and with simplest tools, I'd say not at all.

Exhibitors had a program to sell and did it the cheapest and most efficient way they could. Effective advertising, in fact, had to be a show in itself. There wasn't time to finesse ads to perfection, this a limit most keenly felt in smaller towns where the bill might change three times in a week. Snapping jaw of deadlines kept staff toiling late over shears and glue pot to lay out a next day's promotion. Ads done halfway right needed two hours at least to compose, these wrought from art, graphics, tag lining, much of it borrowed from pressbooks—softcover magazine-style collections of ads of all sizes and short articles about production to be inserted straight into newspapers— courtesy the film company. But these ads were generic by nature. Sometimes an ad composer would rely completely on his or her own imagination to sell a movie. From such detour often came magic.

Showmen had to put hard sell on product they, for a most part, hadn't seen—and yes, product was all that movies were to many, if not most, exhibitors. Those celluloid cans arrived after promise of pleasure had been made to customers, leaving staff to hope a show would meet expectations created by ads. On occasion of letdown (the Classic Era didn't always yield classics), a manager might spend days ducking glare of neighbors whose entertaining night out had proved to be anything but.

Newspapers were the best way to relay the movie message through most of Hollywood's first century. Radio in time became an effective adjunct where used properly, television emerging in the '50s as a most reliable sales partner. Print promotion was second only to word of mouth, but the latter moved slower, and a show might be over and gone before pleased patronage could inform friends. A hit movie that stayed 12 weeks in an urban center often left after one or two days at a corn-belt Bijou.

A hit feature would get thousands of bookings and generate bushels of advertising. United Artists' all-time record holder, 1957's *Thunder Road*, totaled up 34,301 dates at U.S. theatres and drive-ins. From these came ads of infinite number, no two alike, each exhibitor with his or her own idea of how best to sell *Thunder Road*. Some, if not much, of effort was rushed and slipshod. Ads cost money, and that would limit size of an artist's canvas. Time was at premium where a next change breathed down necks of management. Heavy circulation of *Thunder Road* eventually left UA and poster exchanges slap out of advertising stock. Theatres playing it by the mid-'60s, particularly in the South where *Thunder Road* became something of a cultural phenomenon, couldn't beg/borrow accessories long since used up.

Movie posters, lobby cards, etc., were for decades considered junk. Not anymore. Cream among them now hammer for tens of thousands at auction. Movie ads, at best surviving from yellowed newspaper, are still regarded as junk. They are too prolific for any archive to confront. Suppose we assumed the task of gathering every ad composed for *Citizen Kane*. History recalls *Kane* as a flop that was shut out of many theatres, but thousands *did* play it, and not just in 1941–42, but again in 1956–57 and thereafter at art and revival houses. How do we fully comprehend Orson Welles' classic, the merchandising of it, and a public's reception since initial release, short of immersion in *Kane*'s ocean of advertising? Answer is . . . we don't.

Posters valued so highly today came in finite number. There were one-sheets (27" x 41"), occasionally as many as four styles, a set of lobby cards (each 11" x 14"), of which came eight, notwithstanding so-called jumbo cards for special attractions. Larger and varied displays could be had, accessories for a show with higher profile, but there was always a limit to posters a theatre could access. Newspaper ads, on the other hand, saw no limit in variety and number. Promotion of movies at local level could be eccentric to say the least, a sometimes cracked mirror held to showmen whose voice was expressed by ads.

Theatre ads remain less than a footnote to motion pictures' past. They were always a disposable commodity, even to those who designed them. "As transitory as skywriting," said one veteran of the layout bench. An ad's mission was to deliver its message

Citizen Kane (1942)

The Magnificent Ambersons wasn't the only Welles classic to play alongside a Mexican Spitfire, as evidenced by this NYC saturation sub-run. And then there's *Kane* as product for a newsreel theatre, with juke-boxy *Hit Parade of 1943* in support.

The Red Sea parts twice a day for this biggest of DeMille specials and one he'd remake three decades later.

quickly, then disappear like, well, yesterday's newspaper. Who'd want to save them outside of management, who might use spent ads later for reference or guidance?

Vintage ads have a low survival rate. Yes, there are ones that turn up on eBay or clean-out of hoarder houses, but that's a mere fraction of what newspapers generated over a past century. The great purge that took place when libraries converted print archives to microfilm would decimate backlog of dailies preserved as bound volumes, these thought to clog space better used otherwise. Visual integrity of ads, indeed of all printed matter, would be utterly lost to the smear and ugliness that was primitive microfilm. Nationwide conversion from a stable, if fragile, medium to another so vastly inferior, was epic misjudgment on the part of those entrusted to preserve our past.

The result of foregoing and other neglect was history forgetting the showman as artist. Few of these would toot their own horn. Trade magazines might applaud exceptional work, and yes, there were names that stood high in exhibition circles for mastery at layout and salesmanship, but who remembers Frank Whitbeck of the Fox West Coast division, Eddie Hitchcock with Warner Bros.' advertising department in Philadelphia, or Ken Long, whose ad ideas were pride and joy of the Paramount Publix chain? A capable enough exhibitor with finger upon a public's pulse might translate ad

3

expertise to the actual making of movies, as was case for Nat Holt, Fox's city manager in Wichita, who'd go on to produce westerns in partnership with star Randolph Scott, followed by success at series television. A man like Holt knew what sold, having served with distinction in the ad-man's army.

Some exhibitors kept scrapbooks of proud ad accomplishment, from which they shared ideas with colleagues who needed inspiration. The showmanship community was at all times generous, membership eager to help one another at mutual task of luring an audience. One manager's clever ad approach would go viral, as it were, among neighboring towns or states always on lookout for a concept that sold tickets. An exhibitor who rang the bell ad-wise and forwarded winning ideas could depend on meal and drink tabs to be picked up by grateful brother showmen at a next sales convention or managers' meet.

Laying out ads was no glamorous life, being work many performed in addition to tearing tickets, sweeping floors, and hoisting film cans up flight of stairs to the booth, projection yet another job covered in event of employee no-show. Composing an ad for most managers was task piled atop multitude of others, art at best a happenstance from routine so harried. Small town or neighborhood addresses had none of Madison Avenue's glamour, as ad prep stayed barely ahead of newspapers going to press. Romance of Hollywood and the movies was planets away from those who cut and pasted promotion at grass-root level. It fell upon such humble lot to sell shows, good or bad, and capture attention, at best fleeting, of whoever looked at newspapers the next day.

Daily readers were of distracted bent, as television viewers and online surfers later would be. They'd skim articles or ignore them, eyes pin-balling off ads that begged for a moment's attention. Advertising was generally as negligible to readership as the newspaper itself after a quick pass. Showmen sometimes wondered why they should run ads at all, though worse policy would be to discontinue them and surrender ground to competitors. The object, then, was to seize control of printed real estate and within those column inches seduce readership into attending your program rather than others crowded onto a newspaper's Amusement Page.

There was a science to creating ads, at least ones that were effective. Certain of showmen had the gift for layout and copy, while others could generate no stronger work after 20 years of effort than in a first. There are ads you could look at today and wonder why anyone could care about the largely vanished process, then along comes a specimen of such beauty and imagination as to inspire a book like the one you're holding. It came down simply to dedication and effort applied to the job. A lot of ad men performed theirs in rote manner, as was and remains the case with any field of endeavor. Sometimes lazy effort would be called out in trade columns, all toward teaching others how *not* to create an ad. Large circuits or theatres owned by the major film companies kept management on a short leash. Ads from each were scrutinized by the home office, with no quarter given for sloppy result. A man not equal to the task of competitive selling in newspapers would not stay long in his job.

Mildred Pierce (1945)

A selling tag that became a national catchphrase, at least for a few months in 1945: Don't Tell Anyone What Mildred Pierce Did!

Then, of course, there were true creatives. Ones who breathed rarefied air of exploitation and saw layout as Renaissance canvasses. They set a pace that others would follow, recognition measured by how soon their approach was copied by competitors. In days of multiple theatres hustling after the same coin, they had to watch closely what rivals were up to. One ad man described himself as "a pilot flying over very rugged terrain that was the Amusement Page." Introducing fresh approach to ads was fine, but one could not rest on laurels long, for what was fresh last week would atrophy in the wake of imitation.

Hard sell was permissible and, in fact, expected by a public made sophisticated by lifetime exposure to advertising. "Best and Funniest Andy Hardy Yet!" was part and parcel of all entries from the venerable series, and a next performance by Bette Davis or Greta Garbo would naturally be her finest ever. For all of hyperbole spent on ads, there still was trust that had to be maintained by exhibitors vis-à-vis their patrons, many of whom, especially in smaller situations, were personal friends. An ad could exaggerate, but never lie outright. It wouldn't do to borrow art from one movie to advertise another. Title changes were chancy, as was peddling an old film as something brand new. Less-than-honest exhibitors in 1957 sold a Soviet-made cartoon feature called *The Snow Queen* as Walt Disney's *The Snow Queen*, a deception enabled by the import's overlap with Disney formula and use of Tommy Kirk (a popular Disney player) as voice artist. This was a risky sort of flim-flam, as audiences once fooled were loath to forgive or forget.

"Clean" selling was also a priority, at least for theatre chains wanting to avoid flap over hot promotion that might arouse parents and clergy or, worse yet, shut advertising out of local newspapers. The since-celebrated pre-Code era of the early '30s skated nimbly upon the edge of public acceptance, sometimes tipped over, then had to right itself via clean-up of ads in response to protest, only to again test limits once the heat was off. This was motion picture advertising that readers understood and, for the most part, accepted. The object of ads, after all, was to titillate; people then, as now, enjoyed being titillated.

A theatre could promote elements other than movies, some of these more alluring than what was shown on screens. Comfort could attract, as in soft or rocking chairs. Air-conditioning might be reason alone to attend theatres in summer months where temperatures outside were past endurance and few

My Favorite Blonde (1942)

Thought balloons were a surest way to convey laugh content of *My Favorite Blonde*.

homes offered refuge of cool air. Baby-sitting was welcome aspect of Saturday shows that kept youngsters amused through a long day out from under parents' feet. Drive-ins were immensely popular for option of casual dress (goers could attend barefoot or in pajamas if so inclined), and full-service canteens had menu selection way beyond popcorn or candy that was limit to most indoor concessions. All of such benefits were emphasized in ads that often put them first over films being screened.

Partnership with other merchants was a byword for showmen. If a water heater could sell a movie, then movies could surely sell a water heater. Tie-ins with bookstores, hardware suppliers, grocers, record and sheet music stands, a whole of retail selling that orbited the picture house—these and more such relationships drove sales to advantage of businesses that took part. Co-op ads saw expense shared by the theatre and sponsoring retailer, or greater combination of same that participated in ballyhoo for a movie that had potential to fill seats at night and store aisles the next day.

Classic rules for effective advertising were hammered home by counselors to the trade, these being old-timers plus youthful progressives, who'd share how-to with exhibitors newer to the show world. Insider periodicals aimed at management arrived weekly, some daily, and often ran to a hundred or more pages. None went without advice columns or lengthier tutorial on ad layout and pitfalls to avoid when promoting a show. "House organs" published by film companies that also owned theatres put sharper edge to instruction and made mandatory those ad policies developed by the home office. Creative imagination was encouraged among staff at local level, but managers drawing pay from Paramount Publix, Fox West Coast, or others that numbered theatre ownership by the hundreds knew better than to depart radically from guidelines set down by always-observant regional or headquarter bosses.

Vertically integrated companies were ones that produced, distributed, and exhibited movies. There were five such monoliths to scoop much of gravy from ticket windows: Paramount (the largest theatre owner), Fox, RKO, Warner Bros., and Loew's, which was the parent company of MGM. (Universal, Columbia, and United Artists also produced and distributed but did not pursue wide ownership of theatres.) The "Big Five" were flush beside an independent showman who had to make weekly payroll

20 Million Miles to Earth (1957)

Fights and frights combine with outreach to sport fans who might also gravitate to a latest science-fiction bill.

on his own and front the cost for newspaper ads. Large artist staffs worked full-time for the majors, and much was spent on national campaigns. Outside advertising agencies also were used where needed. To such enormous enterprise money seemed no object, even in Depression years when many small theatres were forced to close doors.

Showmen who survived would rely on creative instinct and capacity for what seemed to be nonstop work. All decisions were based on economy, particularly where it came to advertising. Too much spent with the newspaper spelled loss, even where the movie drew well as result of ads. It all came down to apportion of resource. A manager would estimate the potential gross of a film and commit a percentage to advertising, usually three to four percent or perhaps five percent for a first-run attraction that merited it. Outlay would cover not only dollars used for print ads, but cost of posters and other accessories to bally the show. It was a wise exhibitor who stuck to limits for promotion. Many a frugal showman ran no more than small and simple weekly ads in local press, with show titles and playdates the full extent of ballyhoo.

Child Brides (1944)

"Insidious" and "evil," yes, but try keeping customers away from this lurid show at Chicago's Studio Theatre.

For managers able and willing to participate, an ad was daily challenge to fill blank space with arresting content that would stop the "bird in flight" that was readership eyes. As movies became more sophisticated, so did bolster for them. Advances made in printing and image reproduction were a help, as was rise of the star system and use of popular faces to sell seats for a newest release. Perusal of ads from the teens and into the 1920s reflects progress by leaps, as theatres learned how best to merchandise a show and compete with one another. Assured and effective techniques were firmly in place by the 1930s, a style that would serve four essential elements of a movie ad done well: Harmony (elements that do not clash), Clarity (ease of reading and understanding), Unity (overall relationship), and Sequence (easy, natural copy flow).

These were mere labels for instinct that guided the most capable of ad artists. Skill with layout and copy (being fewest words needed to boost a show) was hard-won from experience and a developing sense of what worked and what did not. No genius with ads was born overnight. Beginners tended to make those same mistakes the trades warned against—too-crowded space, wrong emphasis, off-balance design. These were what came of dropout from Harmony, Clarity, et al. Salvation might take the form of an old-timer who'd impart wisdom to beginners on staff. Close study of ads that clicked in the past could help too. Selling a show was not unlike movies Hollywood supplied to theatres, best policy to apply a little, but never too much, originality.

It was essential to know how readership looked at ads, human nature being an eternal and predictable thing (study of this and "mass psychology" was recommended by advisors within the trade). Chemistry was simple, with rules absolute. First off was the focal point of any ad, called the "optical center." It occupied not the exact mathematical center, but an area slightly above it. Then came the matter of how people read—left to right—and from the upper left corner. Some in exhibition went a career not realizing this or, at the least, failing to apply its lessons. Such common sense was ingrained in some, hard learned by others. Another bedrock rule: Illustration used in ads should face in. Never have a figure on the right or left looking also in that direction. The reader would follow his or her sight line right out of the ad and probably not come back.

Any number of visual potions could make an ad magnetic: alphabet shapes, arrows (multiple of these for a double feature plus shorts), triangles, ovals, the time-honored "bull's-eye"—all were weapons against staid or listless promotion. Clever use of them would stop a skimmer and command his or her focus. The classic "S" curve, regular or reversed, was route over which attention could glide from upper corner of an ad to its opposite at the bottom, the reader absorbing all the ad's message in a manner that pleased. Here was salesmanship that knew reading instincts and how to manipulate them.

That bird in flight was fragile, however. Squeeze too tight and it was choked, this the risk of cluttered ads or ones that oversold product. An ad's essential message must always come first. Lose sight of that and the bird would surely fly to a rival's nest.

Such basic guideline was Priority One. No layout, however creative, was any good unless it sold the show. That's where Clarity factored in. An artist with time and budget might impart genius to the Amusement Page, but ads weren't there merely to impress. The idea was to get readers off couch or subway seats and into theatre rows. Old Masters among showmen had to achieve this every time they picked up brush—or scissors.

Lionel Hampton (1944)

Choose from swing or monsters for impetus to attend the Cleveland Palace's stage-screen parlay.

A "show" in the Classic Era was made of many elements. There was the feature, often (if not usually) offered in pairs, double features being dominant after the mid-'30s at most locales. To such meal was added short subjects: a cartoon, comedy, sport reel, serial chapter, travelogue; it could be one, two, any combination of these. A complete program might run three hours and contain four or five "units" to hopeful satisfaction. A manager's job was to let his public know in advance what joys awaited. Why run a Mickey Mouse or Laurel and Hardy, but not mention them in the ad? On-the-fence patronage might succumb just for knowing their favorite comic was on tap or that war footage in a latest newsreel might afford glimpse of a friend or family member.

Just whom did ads address? Any showman would say the whole family; at least that was goal and expectation. Understood was the fact that women read ads more attentively than men and wielded the greater influence as to which shows a family or couple would attend. Children of a household cast votes as well. That's where ad push of a Popeye or Three Stooges might pay. Each family member had a reason for wanting to attend movies. It was up to showmen to address them all with promise of a night out with something for everyone.

Movies were not the only commodity for theatres. Live talent and stage shows were oft attraction at venues large and small. Vaudeville had been an early host to film at a turn of the century, single-reel subjects placed between wire walkers, dog acts, or whatever amused on stage. Positions would be reversed when movies later supplanted vaudeville. Now, it would be wire walkers and dog acts as live support to feature films. A big enough name in person, however, could relegate the screen portion of a show to corner or lowered position on ads. It was simply a matter of weighing appeal of one element against another. Comedians, singers and swing bands, picture stars appearing in playlets or just giving crowds opportunity to glimpse them live—these were stuff to fill seating by thousands, ads beating advance drums to excite attendance.

The show world was ever changing and even convulsive at times. Inevitably came transitions to upend routine and revitalize a tired pastime. Arrival of talking pictures in the late '20s swelled curiosity and crowds, theatre ads shouting to match volume they'd hear on the screen. "Garbo Talks!" or "Hear Harold Lloyd!" were succinct and got seat-filling jobs done. Then arrived a Great Depression and resultant slump.

Mammy (1930)

Talking pioneer Al Jolson still corking up as his starring success with sound begins winding down.

Ads needed baser lure to separate patronage from dimes harder got, and so came "unclean" ads to bestir protest and, in some cases, civic action. War, as in WWII, was hell, but not for theatres. Going to movies reached a peak during the early to mid '40s, and it seemed gravy would forever flow. The postwar downturn some saw coming was a most unwelcome of transitions so far.

Bardot Love Fest (1958)

A Manhattan art house heats up to welcome France's steamiest export, Brigitte Bardot, most popular by far of Euro sex symbols.

Television was for struggling theatres a coup de grâce. A lot of them could no longer afford to advertise effectively and so, with viewing now free at home, closed altogether. Those that sustained got brief hypo from exotic screen processes meant to combat TV. Cinemascope, 3-D, and other widescreen processes, stereophonic sound— these lent well to extravagant advertising, and ads were for a while invigorated by the carnival aspect of BIGGER, WIDER, DEEPER pictures being offered. It was like a second coming of talkies, this latest of novelties fated to burn off as fast.

Television would for a most part push movie ads off the Amusement Page. Film companies found it more efficient and economical to open their product wide, either by region or, eventually, nationwide. Advertising saturation on TV would begin 10 days, a week, or less, ahead of playdates. Home screens penetrating all parts of the

United States by the mid-1950s made newspaper ads a less critical means of promoting. As Hollywood's Classic Era wound down, so did usefulness of print ads. For most situations today, it is enough merely to list feature titles and start times. Effort beyond this in print would be superfluous and an undue expense, what with digital delivery of info and where/when movies can be seen.

This, then, leaves only a past. Movie ads as once constituted are gone and have no prospect for coming back. Those of us who recall crowded Amusement Pages might lament the loss and seek out a book like this for nostalgic reflection, but that alone wouldn't justify compiling it. Theatre ads at their best pioneered a modern science of persuasion that would develop through the twentieth century. They'd be inspired by devices used to sell other products but had structure and discipline all their own. The narrow purpose of movie ads didn't allow for an avant-garde as permitted in fine art, other forms of advertising, or even movie posters from time to time. Print ads had not the space to experiment, what with having to spell out essentials of what, when, where before attention drifted or a page was turned.

Few of those who laid out ads and forgot it the next day could imagine a successor generation that would recognize their creativity and call the result art. That this book missed, for the most part, lifetimes of those whose work it celebrates, is a regret in part relieved by well-drawn film ads having fulfilled their purpose at the time, which was to fill theatres to dollar-making capacity.

Let our sampling, then, speak for these showmen who were artists, but seldom knew it.

Take Care of My Little Girl (1951)

A loaded stage bill to which the film plays second fiddle.

The Unseen (1945)

Vaudeville still a main ingredient for some venues as late as the mid-'40s, as here for the Victory Theatre in Tampa, Florida.

Silents to 1930s

Daily Survival of the Fittest

The Movies Begin
and So Does Ad Competition

Movies got their U.S. start as a novelty assist to vaudeville, early occasion for screen projection at Koster and Bial's Theatre on April 23, 1896. Press coverage gave better publicity than ads could buy. Mere mention of the "Bioscope" among performer lineup was adequate to let vaude watchers know that a new kind of entertainment had arrived. For the first few months, Koster and Bial had the miracle to themselves, their deal with supplier Thomas Edison exclusive for present, but there were others looking to share bounty of the full houses drawn by K&B.

Enter B.F. Keith, major player at vaudeville and not one to abide money flowing other than to theatres he controlled. Keith would introduce competition to movie advertising, his Union Square Theatre offering French views filmed by the Lumiere Brothers. "The real thing" that was "Europe's sensation" was promised by newspaper ads during the week prior to a June 29 open at Union Square. Edison's Vitascope would by implication pale beside the rage of "every European capital" now poised to become "the talk of New York."

Keith applied a show world's oldest maxim to movies: Top the other fellow's advertising with your own. Exhibitors in the coming century would follow his example.

**Koster & Bial's and
Keith Union Square Theatre**

They don't look like movie houses we'd come to know, but these vaudeville addresses first projected films in the United States. Vitascope and Cinematographe would go head-to-head in summer 1896 at, respectively, Koster & Bial's Music Hall and B.F. Keith's Union Square Theatre.

Amusements.

THE REAL THING!

First Exhibition in America of

EUROPE'SSENSATION

LUMIERE'S CINEMATOGRAPHE KEITH'S,

☞ NEXT MONDAY, JUNE 29.

This marvellous invention, realizing the perfection of instantaneous photography, is at present the sensation of every European capital. It is the ORIGINAL CINEMATOGRAPHE, portraying scenes from life and PHOTOGRAPHING MOTION. It will be the talk of New York. See Sunday papers.

←

B.F. Keith

Crudely done, but a first. Run-on and off-center copy introduces the concept of competition among movie ads in print. That finger points to a future in promotion that would employ arrows, shooting stars, and yes, more fingers directing reader attention to theatre offerings.

Ads for Silents Had to Speak

There's misconception even today that "silent" film presentation was quiet as tombs. In fact, the largest of theatres with home-grown orchestras could give present-day cacophony a run for the money. All silent movies really lacked was dialogue. What they had in spades was music and sound effects of infinite variety, especially at venues where performance amounted to far more than mere throw of light upon a screen.

Ads did the talking for that pre-speech era. You'd not get jazz from a soundtrack, but live accompany would easily fill the void, so yes, there were "musicals" before music was recorded for film. Comedy didn't need dialogue because of laughter that filled auditoriums. Advertising could promise, and then deliver, waves of communal joy with a new Harold Lloyd or Charlie Chaplin. Audiences were less inhibited in days before chat that made them stay quiet and listen. A crowd could fairly burst at seams of joy, what with a screen plus live accompany to excite them.

Ads from movies' beginning through the 1920s made more direct appeal to emotion. Are we poorer for having lost that? A star system emerged where names began to mean something, ads charting best a player's rise in public estimation. Fan magazines could monitor popularity of a film or star from month to month, but ads coming day to day were like ticker tape off a fast-paced marketplace that was movies. Rankings were best learned by close observance of Amusement Pages that reflected most accurately what people wanted to see.

→

Charlie Chaplin at Waldorf (1915)

He's coming to the Waldorf, and that's all you needed to know. What other pioneer star was so immediately recognizable, even from the rear? Some ads would go further and omit Chaplin's name—just his image, front or back, would do. The comedian's salary skyrocket got nods as well; if Charlie was worth so much to producers, then he must merit your nickel.

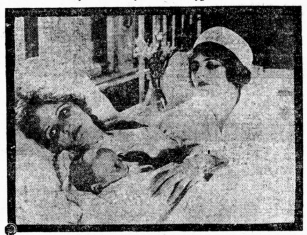

Although This Powerful Photoplay Deals in Bold and Frank Terms With One of the Most Unsavory Problems of Life—Yet There Is a Sweetness and Purity That Pervades the Story Like the Smell of Fresh Roses

LA SALLE
THEATRE Madison Nr. La Salle
STARTING TODAY
CHILDREN UNDER 14 NOT ADMITTED UNLESS ACCOMPANIED BY PARENTS

An Evil Can Never Be Stamped Out by Being Afraid to Talk About It. Plain Speech Must Be Employed When the Dreadful Havoc Caused by Sex Indiscretion Is Discussed. Words Are Not Minced in This Commanding Story

THE MOST WIDELY DISCUSSED PHOTODRAMA OF THE DAY

The Gigantic Dramatic Upheaval

That is awakening a whole nation to the danger that lurks in our vast ignorance upon the subject of Sex Hygiene

Authorized by United States Public Health Service
PUBLIC HEALTH FILMS
PRESENT
THE END OF THE ROAD
PRESENTED BY A WONDERFUL CAST, HEADED BY
RICHARD BENNETT
Famous Star of "DAMAGED GOODS," and
CLAIRE ADAMS

An Enthralling Story of the Diverging Paths of Two Beautiful Girls— One Drifting to the Primrose Path and Its Ensnaring Tragedies—and the Other to a Life of Usefulness and Virtue

Are You Afraid to Tell Your Daughters of the Risk They Run Through Indiscreet Contact With Dissipated Young Men?

One girl was warned by her mother against indiscreet contact with young men, while the other was left in ignorance and she falls an easy prey to a degenerate and a libertine.

Claire Adams, who possesses a personality of rare sweetness and beauty, portrays with exceptional charm a girl who from childhood was taught the fundamentals of right living. She travels along the road of life, spreading her wholesome influence wherever she goes. Playing opposite to Miss Adams is Richard Bennett, one of the best-known actors in this country, who gives a performance of the hero in a most impressive way.

Contrast the Fate of the Girl Kept in Ignorance and the Other Girl Who Was Forewarned by Her Mother of Life's Pitfalls

PRICES:
CONTINUOUS 10:30 A. M. TO 11:00 P. M.

MATINEES (10:30 a.m. to 6 p.m.) 25c AND 50c
NIGHTS (6 p.m. to 11 p.m.) 50c AND 75c (Box Seats $1.00)

←

The End of the Road (1915)

Lock up your daughters! Better still, bring them to what was sternest warning against "ignorance" of sex matters that led invariably to sex "indiscretion." Such was code to confer dignity upon purest exploitation. Yes, *The End of the Road* would address "the most unsavory problems of life," but "with sweetness and purity that pervades the story like the smell of fresh roses." This blossom at Chicago's La Salle Theatre could be sniffed only by youth in the accompany of parents, it being understood by all that *The End of the Road* was s-e-x to minimizing of all else. Public Health Films as producing entity offered scent of reason and responsibility, but most would buy tickets for a look-in at girls set upon a "primrose path," the result of "indiscreet contact with dissipated young men." La Salle copy deftly treads the ridge between public service and censurable content. Could anyone object to theatre effort at the cleansing of youth? Ad avoidance of sex imagery might be noted, though readers figured *The End of the Road* would depict a likely teenaged and undoubtedly single girl being bed bound and baby burdened. It was for patronage to come and view "the gigantic dramatic upheaval" that got her there.

The Birth of a Nation (1915)

First-run ads for *The Birth of a Nation* tended toward austere, being more announcement of show times and theatre policy than ballyhoo for the D.W. Griffith epic. A bull's-eye center featured the title, with surrounding recount of people, horses, scenes, and cost to underline size of the attraction. The Berchel Theatre in Des Moines, Iowa, conveys urgency to attend with "4 weeks in advance" tickets, along with assurance via the *Des Moines Capital* that there have been no riots from the showing. Front-of-house unrest and civil disobedience in other cities playing *Birth* made showmen jittery, but few would resist this mightiest of crowd lures. Note Berchel bid to head off local objection with promise of even-handed depiction of reconstruction: "Scenes of 'carpetbagger' days reflect upon whites as much as negroes." *The Birth of a Nation* aroused passionate debate from the day it opened, the controversy still in play despite a century's passage.

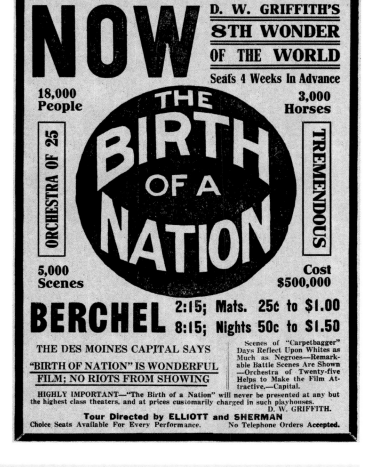

Where Are My Children? (1916)

A raised fist of public outrage signals the coming of a bold attack upon what were then the crimes of abortion and birth control. Advertising's position is made clear, even as the film itself took more subdued measure of issues involved. *Where Are My Children?* ran into censor trouble but played like house afire to record attendance. The 1916 film is available on DVD, which makes for interesting comparison between this highly confrontational ad and what actually showed on-screen.

←

Izzit Charlie Chaplin? (1917)

Sometimes it was fun being fooled. Ersatz Chaplins began appearing within months of the real thing's ascension in 1914. This one was named Billy West, his the most uncanny impression of the lot. Bijou management cleverly makes this a guessing game: Izzit or izzit not Charlie? We can assume film rentals to be less for West, his better reels not appreciably less funny than the McCoy, so crowds could exit for the most part happy. But don't turn the page before noting the young man standing behind Billy West. It's starting-out Babe Hardy playing the "heavy" while a decade away from immortal teaming with Stan Laurel.

→

Cleopatra (1917)

Her man lies supine as vampiress Theda Barà hovers. This was positioning known well to a public that, for a while, sought out Bara helpings of "forbidden but now on view" flavor. She'd go stale with overexposure, but the run-up to that decline included one "Stupendous Super-Vampire Photo Spectacle" after another. Theda's forgotten now thanks to all but a couple of her films being lost, leaving only ads like this and recorded memory of those who worshipped at her throne. Latter was clearly the case here, with the Colonial playing *Cleopatra* on two-a-day policy with reserved seats, making this an important attraction for the 1917 season.

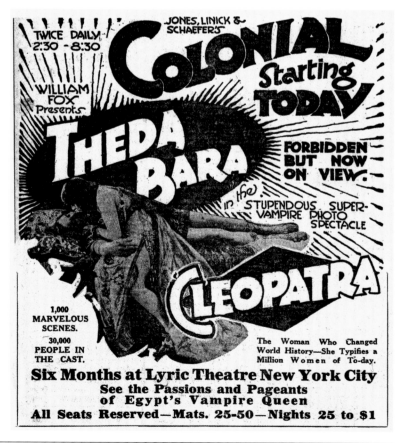

Fanning War Flames

↑

The Greatest War Pictures (1918)

Live lecturers were not unknown during the early silent period. In this instance, one was necessary to explain "The Greatest War Pictures" on view at the Auditorium Theatre in Saginaw, Michigan. These programs came under heading of public service and educational opportunity for youth, sentiment being that if this war lasted long enough, many of them would be called upon to serve. "Germany's great howitzer" represents salesmanship amidst the learning, ad readers assured they'd get a thrill for the display of firepower that was part/parcel of modern warfare.

→

To Hell with the Kaiser (1918)

Toward slamming your point home, here's a two-column jab for two-theatre play of *To Hell with the Kaiser*, a 1918 kiss blown to our German opponents during the Great War. An exclamation point was initially affixed to the title, as if one were needed. Much hissing and profanity was loosed among viewers where these atrocity features ran, the idea being to raise recruits, keep home fires hot, and lobby-sell Liberty Bonds in the bargain. Use of such an indelicate title was excused by wartime conditions—a WWII counterpart would be called *The Devil with Hitler*.

←

Try to Get In (1918)

Under a heading of challenge to your public, here was an audacious ad placed by theatres using Fox Film product for the 1918–19 season. Someone was pioneering in audience psychology. "Super excellence" was assured with stars of this caliber on hand: Theda Bara, vamp favorite (still a pin-up girl in old movie books), William Farnum, a dinosaur who would defy extinction by working years into talkers, and Evelyn Nesbit, noted for involvement in a real-life killing. These were names with which to conjure as a world war wound down, that goal met with assist of *The Prussian Cur* and *Why America Will Win*. Note the ad's flattery of Fox film patronage, many in uniform or formal attire. The finest pictures were not to be viewed in casual dress. Question then: What portion of 1918 attendees actually turned out in top hat and tails?

←

The Romance of Tarzan (1918)

About as sophisticated and accomplished as ads had become by 1918 was this product of the Loew's chain of theatres. Loew's had art staff to keep competition nicely in the shade. The 1,800-seat Stillman was the pride of Cleveland, the city's largest theatrical venue to that time. Elmo Lincoln had played Tarzan once, would do so again and be remembered best as the barrel-chested Ape Man. Tarzan as "love epic" was means by which these early jungle adventures were sold to adults as well as excited youngsters. MGM went a similar route with its talkie series in the early '30s. It was only later that the character would be slanted toward juveniles, eventually winding ways down to cartoon retelling by Disney. Note the ad's use of silhouette jungle to surround the lovers within. Film ads had come a long way since primitive beginnings.

↑
Why Change Your Wife? (1920)

"Intimate real-life action" as conducted in marital beds was by 1920 a known quantity from C.B. DeMille, the director who'd tickle, yet ultimately reinforce the sanctity of wedded vows. Note Milwaukee's Modjeska Theatre tipping off the dénouement of *Why Change Your Wife?* ("—the wife won in the end!!"), only suspense for a paying audience being how she'd do it. Extravagantly gowned Gloria Swanson is erotic lure for erring husband Thomas Meighan, and ad onlookers. The art alone would snare ticket buyers curious as to "the man's side of modern marriage."

↑
Oh, You Women (1919)

Odd seeming to us today is the policy of detailing a film's story in promotional ads, and yet it was commonplace in an era when narrative was often a challenge to follow. Or maybe this was accommodation to readers who wanted to know exactly what they'd get for the price of admission. Either way, there'd be no surprises for an audience settling down to watch *Oh, You Women* at the Crescent.

→

Flying Pat (1920)

Manager J.A. Partington refers to his Portola
Theatre in San Francisco as "The House of
Mirth," this probably not the first week he had
banished "doleful moments." Theatres were
best, and most profitably, designated as sites for
gaiety. Partington's Mr. and Mrs. Patronage will
achieve "heights of happiness" not only from the
voiceless exploits of Dorothy Gish as *Flying Pat*,
but a Mack Sennett comedy plus Portola resident
singer Helene Hughes and "lively concerts"
from what was presumably the Portola's house
orchestra.

→

Ruth of the Rockies (1920)

It's easy to forget how enormously popular serials
were during a silent era. They weren't just for
kids as later would be the case. Newspapers ran
plot summaries that per week followed progress
shown on screens, and grown-ups read those
avidly, especially women for whom a Ruth Roland
(or Pearl White, or Helen Holmes) were role models. This ad sells the sensation well: Ruth and
mount look ready to plunge an abyss, but rest
assured they'll be back next week. These early
chapter-plays lasted months and would extend
even beyond that when showmen asked for more
chapters. Ruth and kin, scorning doubles, really
were plucked from the roofs of speeding boxcars,
plunged off aeroplanes into the drink, and so
forth. Gone are the thrills.

→

A Child for Sale (1920)

The '20s was as child-centered an era as our present day, if ads such as these are indication. "Dramatic thunderbolt" *A Child for Sale* told the story of a widowed father who must barter one offspring in order to feed the other. Such a blow was softened for Strand audiences by the Blanche Hertz Kiddies in live performance, along with Santa Claus bearing boxes of candy for tots in attendance. This was how families were lured to holiday programming at theatres in 1920.

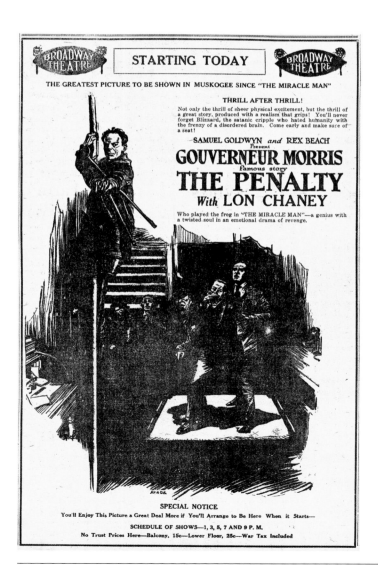

←

The Penalty (1920)

Arresting (and signed) art highlights the Broadway Theatre's Lon Chaney follow-up to twice-mentioned *The Miracle Man*, one that we may assume left a deep impression among the populace of Muskogee, Oklahoma. *The Penalty* came a year later in 1920, and, yes, there was plenty of "sheer physical excitement" courtesy of "satanic cripple" Chaney, who would begin his decade of major stardom here. Note the Broadway's counsel that ticket buyers arrive early so as to ensure a seat, a device in its early application, but one used in decades to come when the attraction merited it (notably 40 years later with Alfred Hitchcock's *Psycho*, a thriller that addressed itself also to "the frenzy of a disordered brain").

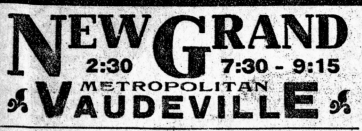

NEW GRAND
2:30   7:30 – 9:15
METROPOLITAN
⚜ VAUDEVILLE ⚜

Beginning TOMORROW, MONDAY, JAN. 6
And Playing Every First
Half Show for
Fifteen Consecutive Weeks

HOUDINI
The World's Greatest
Entertainer, in
The Master Mystery

By ARTHUR B. REEVE and CHAS. A. LOGUE

Don't Fail to See the First Episode
MONDAY, TUESDAY AND WEDNESDAY

NEW SHOW MONDAY
Lovett's "Concentration" Science, Music and Mirth

Gilroy Haynes & Montgomery	BILL ROBINSON
"The Deputy"	Dark Cloud of Joy
MENNING SISTERS	JESS & DELL
Harpists and Violinists	Human Puppets

NEW SHOW THURSDAY
"Tom Brown's Musical Highlanders" A Musical Muse in Kilts
O HANA SAN & CO., AND THREE OTHER STELLAR ACTS.

LAST TIMES SUNDAY—"AN HEIR FOR A NIGHT"; NICK HUFFORD; CHARLES J. HARRIS & CO.; FRANCES DYER; THE DEONZOS.

No Seat Reservations for Night Performances Held After 6 P. M.

→
The Round-Up (1920)

You may already know of the heights from which rotund comedian Roscoe Arbuckle tragically fell. There's not space here to recount the sadness, but perhaps these ads will spur readers to further inquiry, for it's a hypnotic saga. *The Round-Up* was Arbuckle's first feature after years of two-reel mirth making, and, yes, it was apt to call him "The Best Known Fat Man on Earth" as does copyist for the New Fillmore and New Mission Theatres, dual San Francisco hosts for *The Round-Up* during the 1920 holiday season. Note musical aggregations for respective venues, Strachan's Orchestra as accompany at the New Fillmore and Waldemar Lind conducting at the New Mission. These names had meaning for San Franciscans, for if screen entertainment fell short, orchestras could fill the void.

←
The Master Mystery (1920)

Here's fascinating 1920 instance of a special film attraction being used to prop up the bill at a vaudeville house. *The Master Mystery* was a chapter thriller and the picture debut for magician and illusionist Harry Houdini, who was then the object of intense curiosity for apparent supernatural abilities to escape any trap to which he was confined. Many theatres could and did build their program around installments of *The Master Mystery* (the serial is extant and available on DVD). In this New Grand instance it is the stage artists, including "Dark Cloud of Joy" and dancing marvel Bill Robinson, who will retire backstage as Houdini magic is projected, *The Master Mystery* the only film on an otherwise all-live bill. Distinct advantage for any popular serial was a boost of business for those weeks the chapters played, in this case 15. Assuming patrons were hooked from week one, they'd be back for a virtual season to follow, with resulting paid admissions the New Grand could happily rely upon.

↑
The Life of the Party (1921)

Roscoe seems immune to vampish charms played upon him here, and who of amused patronage could imagine he'd face a tribunal for the rape death of a starlet within a year after this happy booking for *The Life of the Party*? His guileless ad expression moves us today for knowledge of what fate had in store, but delighted crowds at the California Theatre did not share our rear view, so they'd be regaled not only by Roscoe, but Baby Boynton, "World's Youngest Organist at the World's Largest Organ" fame. (Really? Well, it's going on a century too late to confirm now.) The California's ad cites the story origin for *Party* as *The Saturday Evening Post*, then the most popular of slick magazines.

←
Lyman H. Howe's Travel Festival (1921)

Lyman Howe was a traveling showman considered best in that crowded field. His programs offered a variety of scenics and spectacle, with Howe himself or informed lecturers offering background for each film subject. Outstanding among his output was the Runaway Train reel, a sensation from 1921 when it first appeared and continuing so for years after. Howe was able to attract upscale audiences thanks to his focus on travel topics and willingness to inform as well as entertain.

←

Dream Street (1921)

Master director D.W. Griffith is alone the reason for attending *Dream Street*, says Majestic Theatre ads from 1921, a year following the triumph of his *Way Down East*. Griffith's face was familiar from magazine profiles and earlier film publicity, so readers who kept abreast of entertainment would know him on sight. Featuring DWG on behalf of *Dream Street* was wisest means by which the Majestic would promote the show.

↑ ↗

The Cabinet of Dr. Caligari (1921)

Dr. Caligari was sufficiently odd a duck as to demand advertising unconventional as the German-imported film itself. Showmen knew in advance that this was not a show for everyone; in fact, most suspected it was not entertainment for *anyone*. There had been picketing at some venues showing *The Cabinet of Dr. Caligari*. The Alamo Theatre in New Orleans headed off furor by frank acknowledgment that *Dr. Caligari* was a mixed bag, as in "Great!" "Rotten!" "Fine!" or plain "I Don't Get It!" Such candor was chancy at best, most patrons preferring amusement over challenge. *The Cabinet of Dr. Caligari* would find its greater audience a few years later at art houses where the film's offbeat content could be better understood and appreciated.

Tol'able David (1921) ↓

The T&D Theatre of Oakland hung ad banners for the "thrill and throb" show of 1921 with art depicting crowds that would surely converge upon doors for the week "commencing tomorrow." *Tol'able David*'s hit status was known ahead of ad preparation, so it risked little to present heavy attendance as a foregone conclusion.

The Bakery (1921) →

Was Larry Semon really "the funniest fellow in the world"? Some—in fact, many—in 1921 thought so; enough anyway for the Alamo Theatre to top-bill the comic's latest. Management must have previewed *The Bakery* to detail its content (Larry's trained animals). His "self-raising uproar of fun" amounted to two short reels, those 25 minutes sufficient to fill Alamo seats, with satire *The Butterfly Girl* a seeming afterthought.

→
The Young Rajah (1922)

Was it properly spelled "Rudolph," or "Rodolph"? Either way, he was "gorgeous," said this ad for New York's Capitol Theatre in its Broadway bow for Valentino's latest, *The Young Rajah*. Gorgeous wasn't a label that future male stars would seek, however appropriate. They'll still shun it for risk of ridicule, which was heaped upon Valentino along with slurs to his manhood. The Capitol was selling its "perfect lover" to women, and enough of them plus men they dragged along would handily fill those 4,000 seats. "Love—Thrills—Beauty" was augmented by the Capitol's orchestra, this the definition of a movie palace as understood then and since. As for Valentino, he'd have but four years left to ply romantic trade before early death claimed him at age 31.

↑
The Primitive Lover (1921)

Here was further instance of a marquee ad featuring crowds surging toward the box office. The additional "Tivoli" front emphasizes the stature of the theatre at which *The Primitive Lover* will unspool, that title, by the way, being catnip for patronage and very much what we'd expect a typical silent drama to be called. But wait: *The Primitive Lover* was a comedy, and its star, Constance Talmadge, was known for laugh making. It was her sister, Norma, who'd troupe mainly in melodrama.

↑

Thrill Chaser (1923)

Westerns by the '20s were a mainstay for neighborhood theatres and smaller towns. There were more of these modest venues than thousand-seater palaces, so cowboys could profit even as they rode less often on urban and first-run landscape. The Beverly featured Hoot Gibson because they knew their audience, even if careless borrowing from Universal's pressbook resulted in copy being repeated here. It was enough to let the mob know that Hoot was back and in accustomed action.

↑
Dante's Inferno (1924)

It promised to be one Hell of a show, what with nudity in the ads (did newspaper hosts complain?), and "more beautiful women than all combined Broadway reviews." Devils with pitchforks in pursuit of naked souls was worm upon hook that crowds would surely bite, and we may assume *Dante's Inferno* stood them in the aisles. Fox would revisit the title and theme for talkies. Anticipation wove around an extended tour of purgatory at its halfway point, either a wake-up from the first half or goose into the second. Either way, this was the portion that guests to the Central Theatre on Broadway would tell their friends about, so it's not a wonder that ad emphasis was placed entirely on this highlight to the exclusion of any cast listing. Management at the Central knew that the Devil would pay.

↓
Baby Peggy in Person (1924)

Baby Peggy would have recently turned six when she made this personal appearance—a six year old stood before thousands daily for a week of repeated shows. *The Family Secret* would be next to last of her starring features. By age seven, she was done in leads, her money spent by parents. The Pantages was Hollywood Boulevard's address for vaudeville and for movies when they'd attract, as here with Baby Peggy on stage and screen. The ad centers its child wonder and leaves the rest as garnishment, Peggy the best if not only reason to attend that week.

↑ ↓ →

Hot Water (1924)

Comedy was a most popular genre during the silent era and endures best for viewers to-day. Harold Lloyd features were looked forward to like the circus coming to town. His was more prolific output than Chaplin, while other laugh makers came nowhere near Lloyd's popularity. *Hot Water* was a 1924 release that would inspire pen-and-ink ad depiction of amusing moments from the film, all that was needed to let Harold's public know that he was back with a fresh "Wow." The *Hot Water* title served as natural for tie-in with local gas and water heat companies, as here with Beloit, Wisconsin's supplier. Merchants everywhere were eager to hitch wagons to the star that was Harold Lloyd.

Also from 1924 came Buster Keaton with *The Navigator*, the now-feature star easily recognized even from behind in the New York Capitol's first-run ad, itself recognition of Keaton as a comedy star of the first rank. *The Navigator* would have a second Broadway run at the Loew's State, that venue under the same corporate ownership as the Capitol. For this occasion they'd spotlight a personal appearance by recent heavyweight champ Jack Dempsey, with *The Navigator* relegated to junior attraction. The ad makes clear that Dempsey was what Loew's State patrons would come to see.

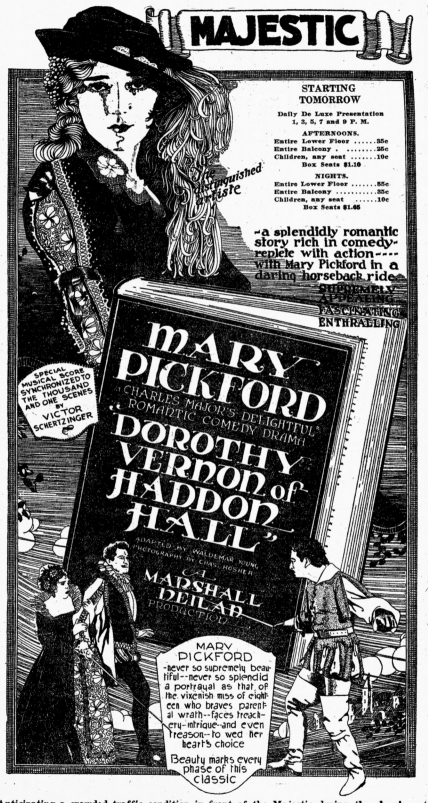

Anticipating a crowded traffic condition in front of the Majestic during the showing of "Dorothy Vernon of Haddon Hall" the police department has ordered the placing of a traffic officer in front of the theater during the entire week.

Dorothy Vernon of Haddon Hall (1924)

Here was what came of a star balloon becoming too inflated. Mary Pickford had been producing her own films for several years by 1924. Each were "events," with theatres obliged to treat them so. The Majestic assures its patronage of police out front to manage crowds, but did that encourage attendance? There was such thing as too much bloom on a rose. Would Little Mary's loyal following prefer her as "the distinguished artiste" as tendered here? Prices were advanced for the "deluxe presentation," in part to recover high rental imposed by United Artists, the distributor owned in part by Pickford. She'd hedge bets by playing "a vixenish miss of eighteen," fourteen years short of the actress' offscreen age. The Majestic, like many such houses in receipt of high-profile star vehicles, rolled dice they were handed. Their ad, at least, was a pen-and-ink masterpiece that *Dorothy Vernon of Haddon Hall* could only hope to match. Did management quietly realize this was not the Mary Pickford their customers preferred to see?

↑

Miss Minneapolis (1924)

Sometimes the biggest stars were local ones, such as here, where home-girl Miss Minneapolis is featured on Pantages' stage before heading to final competition in Atlantic City. Pageant winners in residence were a source of pride for towns large and small, many if not most paraded past footlights to demonstrate beauty, and sometimes talent, for admiring neighbors.

←

Greater Movie Season Contest (1925)

Properly launching a "Greater Movie Season" required commitment greater than random ads. The people had to be made picture-conscious, with theatregoing the stuff of happy memory. Contests would bestir recollection of the most thrilling hours sat before a screen. Who among those who saw Lon Chaney as the Phantom of the Opera would forget him? Many kept that startling image in mind's eye for the rest of their lives, a guessing game here played but a year after the film had arrived to startle a show world. Let's just say the "contest" was no contest for anyone who'd gone to see it, or for many who'd been told what sensations Chaney and his Phantom were.

↑

Greater Movie Season (1925)

Theatres and filmmakers shared a nonstop goal of instilling the movie habit. Better still was making movies a first choice for family recreation. Turnstiles spun happiest to *groups* buying admission, and it was for showmen to customize evenings that would attract any/all ages or preferences. This was years before filmgoing splintered, with certain members targeted to the exclusion of others. "Greater Movie Season" was the shared celebration of moving pictures' thirtieth birthday by a now-vast industry that was beginning to feel the pinch from rival radio. Promotionals sought to get folks away from living rooms and into theatres, not just occasionally but on a weekly or more basis. To stay home or, worse, stay home and be entertained by radio was opposition to be fought. Shabby nickelodeons were dying hard, thus co-op ads assuring that movies were no longer primitive "store shows" of a mere "day before yesterday." To miss movies now was to consign yourself to a "small minority," and who wanted that?

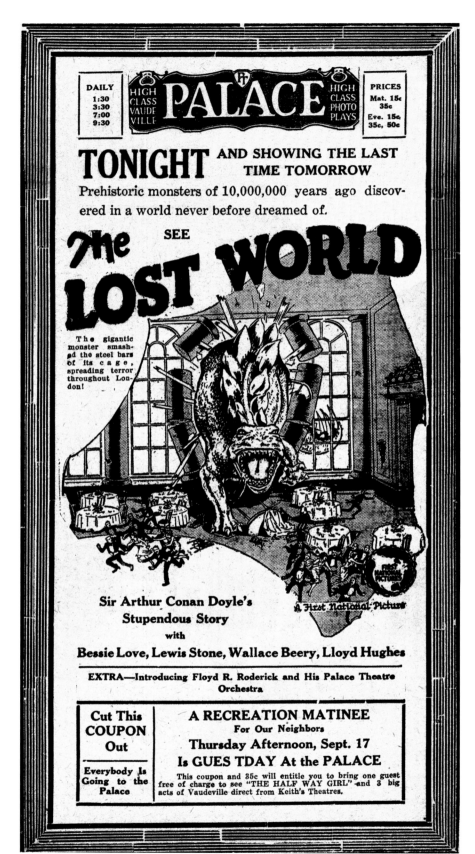

Here was something movies hadn't offered before, the concept not so commonplace as it would later become. Audiences could but wonder how it was all done, some assuming that prehistoric creatures actually had been found and photographed. Showmen liked trick movies for the novelty they could lend to layouts. Cast and content of the show would be secondary to beasts it boasted, exhibitors knowing that curiosity alone would meet house expense for the week or weeks *The Lost World* played.

→

Variety (1926)

Imports were a tough sled during silent days and after. This one was out of Germany, bearer-nation of dubious gift that was *The Cabinet of Dr. Caligari* a few seasons before—and greeted by empty houses if not open derision. Better then to ignore origin other than to emphasize the "international beauty" that was Lya de Putti along with increasingly known (at least among art-housers) Emil Jannings, the latter to become a major star after Paramount brought him over. *Variety* is regarded as a classic now, whereas 1926 saw it more colorfully sold in terms of "love lure," an element foreign product had that we often lacked. Offshore and arty stuff clicked best in urban situations, *Variety* doing well in New York dates, and figured to score for San Francisco's Imperial Theatre. Its ad wisely targets a mainstream, with popular Harry Langdon a comedy bonus for general patronage. Paramount distributed *Variety* in the U.S. and its Publix chain owned the Imperial, so latter's arresting ad may have been home-office generated. It puts across the "spice" of the show, in any case.

↑

The Palm Beach Girl (1926)

The '20s was a sped-up decade: faster cars, boats, trains—the quick-moving lot. Movies too were keyed to speed, as were the best ads promoting them. Rail vs. water is vividly captured in art for *The Palm Beach Girl*, a 1926 vehicle (in every sense of the term) for popular Bebe Daniels. From noise and excitement implied here, you'd almost think *The Palm Beach Girl* came after arrival of sound, not before.

↑

The Devil Horse (1926)

Rex was a wonder horse, a *wonderful* horse by reckoning of millions during the mid to late '20s. He made features, then serials and "B's" with career decline in talkies. Rex was all an ad needed to sell his goods. Toward argument that this steed had everything came claim he "fights like a fiend, loves like a woman, and hates like a man." There were surely more attributes, but who needed them? San Francisco's California Theatre had but so many seats (2,135, in fact), and *The Devil Horse* likely filled them all. Animal action was all a rage during silent days. Why isn't it still? Maybe because there aren't ads with punch like this one. You'd figure *The Devil Horse* for children, but grown-ups loved such things as well, maybe for the fact they were so well produced, with Hal Roach of comedy fame the brains behind Rex. Ad ingenuity at work: *The Devil Horse*-head looking downward at the main body of the ad, and our eyes follow.

New York's Criterion ad for *Wings* was simple in recognition of its public knowing well the sensation this epic of air war was. Paramount spent piles leading up to a roadshow premiere that commanded high admissions and seats sold on reserve basis. The Criterion was for all intent and purpose a legit house in terms of prestige attached to this sprawl of flying action, the theatre utilizing an expanded screen called "Magnascope" to further enhance *Wings*. Two-a-day shows heightened a status that few features would share that season. *Wings* would stay and stay at the Criterion for more than a year, yielding its place to Paramount's first talking feature, *Interference*, on 11/16/28. "Made by men who were war-flyers" proved sound marketing; authenticity was very much *Wings*' raison d'être. There had been screen combat in the air before, but never on such scale. Exhibitors saved the hard-sell drumbeat for attractions that needed it—*Wings* word-of-mouth permitted Criterion ads to be as reserved as those seats the theatre sold at premium price.

→
Nosferatu (1929)

Nosferatu was a vampire thriller from Germany that is still famous. Adapted from *Dracula* in 1922, it wouldn't be seen in the U.S. until a New York art house, the Film Guild, took a chance in June 1929. One trade review called *Nosferatu* "morbid and depressing," and maybe that's just what the Film Guild's following liked. Art houses catered to a rarefied audience, so ads leaned to announcement rather than flash. Still, this was a closest embrace between art and exploitation during 1929, the promise of "blood-lust" widening crowds beyond the Film Guild's egghead base. Was creepy Max Schreck photo-seen for a first time in America with this ad? He'd be immortalized thereafter, his visage familiar yet to those of horrific bent.

↑

A Woman of Affairs (1928) and Wild Orchids (1929)

New-arrived from Sweden, Greta Garbo meant but one thing to most audiences: Hot European Love. Maybe they should have called one of her movies by that title—one was, in fact, titled *Love*. Garbo wore no leash in love scenes. Her clinching with co-star John Gilbert made theatres glad for recently installed air conditioners. It was made clear that GG had not those inhibitions visited upon American women. To sell her was a simple matter of putting the kiss front/center and letting imaginations do the rest. Note her attitude in ads—yielding and ardent. The copy wrote itself, these a virtual thesaurus with which to teach Garbo's art of love. *Languorous, pulsating, searing,* and the rest would quickly be absorbed into filmgoers' vocabulary.

Was Everybody Listening?

Movies were due for sound. In fact, overdue. There had been efforts since Edison to make screens talk. All came a cropper for technical bugs, worst of which was the inability to amplify voices so all in an auditorium could hear. Listeners of radio, their number increasing daily, were getting impatient for aural experience at theatres. Corporate monoliths heard and responded. Electric and telephone brain trusts went to work and allied with film companies ready to roll dice.

Warner Bros. and the Fox Film Corporation were first out of gates, their chat recorded on discs or on the edge of the celluloid itself, respectively. A public being mad for new invention came in numbers unknown to ticket sellers. The picture trade seemed reborn. Announce sound and your house would fill. Crowds would even forgive snafus, breakdowns, voice and image drifting out of sync. We were all in this experiment together.

Ad makers went giddy at receipt of a whole new glossary of superlatives. Hear him talk! Hear her talk! Listen to them all sing! Excitement leapt off Amusement Pages as tide of silence went out and wave of sound came in. That word "talk" (make that TALK) was like flies on honey and magnet to reader eyes. Who'd watch Richard Dix mute when his manly voice now thundered from newly installed amplifiers? The challenge was to make ads talk loud as the movies that had been revolutionized. Exhibition's horn of plenty seemed deep as those horns installed back of screens to give them speech.

Don Juan (1926)

Few theatres were equipped to play the 1926 *Don Juan* with Vitaphone accompaniment, itself limited to music and effects, with no spoken voices. The spectacle of sound would for the present be confined to Warner-owned houses where *Don Juan* made history as a first-ever feature with recorded accompany. Theatres like the Rialto made do with *Don Juan* as conventional silent, popular John Barrymore's "gorgeous sinner" deemed sufficient lure for patronage. In case Mr. Barrymore fell down, there was kid footage from the local Lion Club's Easter egg hunt to pull attendance of at least the moppets shown and their parents, plus whoever was kin or friendly with same. Such "home movies" were excitedly received in smaller communities where audiences could see themselves and call out names of neighbors they'd recognize, this a part of shared delight in attending hometown shows.

←

The Jazz Singer (1927)

Al Jolson conquers New York. *The Jazz Singer* made its Broadway bow on October 6, 1927, with two shows a day at admissions from fifty cents to $2.20. Folks were eager to see *The Jazz Singer*, and perhaps *more* eager to tell their friends that they had seen *The Jazz Singer*. It was that kind of social phenomenon. Word spread of something strange and wonderful happening in movies. Everyone was asking local theatres when *The Jazz Singer* would come, not aware of the effort and expense Vitaphone entailed for showmen installing it. The Warner Theatre varied ads throughout a long run, warning here of long lines, then later of limited time left to see and hear *The Jazz Singer*. That title, plus upper-lower chorus dancing in opposite directions, contrasting images of Jolson in stage blackface and "himself" guise, bespoke the electric experience waiting for crowds coming to *The Jazz Singer*. And came they did.

←

When a Man Loves (1927)

Suddenly everything was secondary to sound. San Francisco made Vitaphone seem a cultural event by center ad placement of tenor Giovanni Martinelli from New York's Metropolitan Opera. Readers might be forgiven for assuming that Martinelli himself would be in performance at the Embassy, but no, it was a Vitaphone short to precede the feature attraction, *When a Man Loves*, a John Barrymore romance that would once again utilize a recorded score, but no spoken words. The laugh-talk-play-sing aspect of Vitaphone was addressed solely by Martinelli and others on the support program. Again, the "Symphony Orchestra of Seventy-Five Musicians" implies a live recital. Audiences accustomed to on-site accompany may have been let down by a mechanical substitute but for novelty that was Vitaphone. Some of them would look back in longing to "silent" days when movies were also a concert event. Screen players that talked would cover the loss, but show-going would not be the same again.

The Jazz Singer (1927/1928)

The Wilson Theatre, of same-named North Carolina town, had opened for vaudeville in 1919 and switched to movies since. They were owned by the Paramount Publix chain, so there was money to reequip for sound. The outreaching Jolson figure announcing that "I have brought Vitaphone to Wilson" was clarion call to locals whose demand was heard by Wilson management and the Publix home office. Study in contrasts: Wilson populace got in for between ten and fifty cents, but had to wait for *The Jazz Singer* and Vitaphone. So did a lot of small towns, some of which didn't get talkies until late 1929 or even 1930. Those theatres that could not afford the switch would eventually close doors.

The Cock-Eyed World (1929)

1929 was a year when folks came to listen more than watch. Smart inter-titles gave way to spoken wisecracks. These tickled edges of propriety where Captain Flagg and Sergeant Quirt (Edmund Lowe and Victor McLaglen) were back from previous smash *What Price Glory?* (1926) to again brawl over dames and drink. *The Cock-Eyed World* was a first for coarse language flung by once silent shadows, and crowds were thrilled by it. Profanity that could only be lip-read before could now be approximated by dialogue more or less true to crude idiom of Marines serving love and war. This ad for New York's Roxy date proposes a "load of laughs" to render *What Price Glory?* "as tame as a bedtime story." Leg art of Lily Damita, both photographic and cartoon-drawn, hammers home sex lure of *The Cock-Eyed World*, a tedious sit today but ginger-a-plenty for 1929 fun seekers.

↑
The Iron Mask (1929)

Some stars came tentative to talking's lectern, among these Douglas Fairbanks, who opined that action should speak louder than words. He completed *The Iron Mask* in silence, then was obliged to add chat, plus a recorded score. By early 1929 release, theatres and their attendance expected favorites to greet them in voice, and as Fairbanks spoke but a brief prologue, copyists had to dance on pinheads of truth in advertising. Note these samples of *The Iron Mask* in subsequent runs, both being spring or later dates when there seemed less excuse for players not talking. Loew's State bids us to "hear Doug speak," but neglects noting to what extent. *The Iron Mask* is tendered as a "sound hit," but fails to reveal its being limited to scored accompany and little else. The Rex Theatre cites music by Dr. Hugo Riesenfeld and is honest by loose definition re Fairbanks talk: He "tells the story's motivation, then portrays it in action," this a tough code to crack by readers wanting to hear as well as see Doug and his musketeers.

↑
Coquette (1929)

Rather than parse truth as with *The Iron Mask,* theatres could brand *Coquette* as "all talking," to the joy of fans who'd get 100 percent speech from Mary Pickford after two decades' silence. Waiting that long to hear a beloved star's voice was like having a mute family member suddenly find words. Ads needed only the Pickford name and all-talking assurance. Mary's *Coquette* performance having set "a new high standard for stage or screen" was the Granada's way of equating talkies with legit drama, a last barrier between film and theatre down at last. A "new" Pickford would be grown-up in speech and manner, the Granada adding "forbidden love and one night in a lonely cabin" to her repertoire. Would Mary's public transfer affection to the reborn modern woman? Answer may have come with her exit from starring roles after 1933.

↑

The Cocoanuts (1929)

With recorded music at last a hometown reality, showmen could boast of Broadway brought to Main Street and put transplanted plays on continuous-run basis. *The Cocoanuts* came early (1929) in the raid-from-stage cycle, ads getting start at "all talking, singing, dancing" and so forth that we associate with tunes turned loose on a moviegoing public, till then fed music by house orchestras, ensemble, or the humble piano accompany. Emphasis for ads was less Marx Bros. than the fact we would hear what New Yorkers did and for less admission (Broadway wasn't staging matinees for a quarter, as would the Majestic Theatre here). We expect advertisers to hammer home a point, but note *four* times the word "dancing" is applied on behalf of *The Cocoanuts*, with "singing" invoked thrice. Such was excitement stirred by the start of movie musicals and ads promoting them.

A Bunch of Liars?

Theatres by talkie arrival had worn out "words of praise," their audience wise to ballyhoo and its embroidery of truth. So as not to come off like "a bunch of liars" about the showing of 1929's *Dynamite*, the Orpheum would rely instead on novelty that was Magnascreen, a come-on that was no more than projector lens switch to enlarge a screen image, with results grainier and less clear. Who knows but that outgoing patrons figured this for *more* deception from the Orpheum's bunch of liars?

←

Nothing But the Truth (1929)

The miracle of talkies was, at times, a thing beyond capacity of ads to describe. They'd even admit it, as here. What was more persuasive than surrender by a seller to power "the screen alone" had? *Nothing But the Truth* and other of earliest all-talkies were thus a supernatural force upon audiences who'd surrender themselves to all talking, singing, howling, and laughing. *Nothing But the Truth* was third of a Granada triad that included *The Wild Party*, which was Clara Bow's first talker, and *Coquette*, Mary Pickford's initial go at sound. These must have been well-received by Granada crowds or else they'd not be referenced. Greatest novelty in the first half of 1929 was ticking off stars as they spoke for a first time, *Nothing But the Truth* being Richard Dix's turn at microphones. "The kind of a voice you expected Dix to have" suggests Granada presence at a trade preview, or having taken a brother showman's word that Dix registered OK for sound, not necessarily the case for other leading men submitted to baptism of fire that was talking pictures (see John Gilbert). Note too a trunkful of short subjects on Granada's bill, an exhausting six. Was there no saturation point for talkie-besotted crowds?

→

Weary River (1929)

A big enough opening would sometimes inspire art of a theatre front as it welcomes patronage, as was the case at the Strand's Easter 1929 run of *Weary River*, a Richard Barthelmess vehicle where he would, among other things, sing for a first time on-screen (the voice dubbed, alas, but that's another story). Again there is emphasis on price difference between this engagement and $2.00 roadshow rates. Also the lure, one used often by theatres through that year, of a "latest and improved" sound system.

←

His Glorious Night (1929)

And so to John Gilbert, a most pitiful casualty of pitiless sound. His voice was fine, or at least seems so to us. Some will maintain it doesn't fit a romantic leading man, and yes, they have a point. Did 1929 recording and playback play a role in Gilbert's oblivion? No problem was apparent when Kansas City, Missouri's Uptown Theatre announced simply that "John Gilbert Talks" in *His Glorious Night*. In view of Gilbert's enormous popularity, no more need be said. The ad was simple, effective, and left white space to show confidence in a star whose mere presence would fill seats. *His Glorious Night* was a success and earned profits. Erosion came with Gilbert follow-ups and what seemed a determination on the part of trade and fan press to take the actor down. His decline remains a mystery not likely to be resolved, as who's left to remember?

↑

The Broadway Melody (1929)

MGM came late to the talkie fray (February 1929), having smoothed sound wrinkles to assure Leo's roar for newly polished talk and song, unlike rivals having stumbled in eagerness to profit off a show-world game changer. *The Broadway Melody* was seen by critics and public as sound done truly right, and its rating a roadshow was understood—this was the mighty MGM after all. Twice a day at raised admissions was OK when the best was being tendered. Said "Big Parade of the Gay White Way" was reference to *The Big Parade*, MGM's earlier hit treatment of the Great War—it always paid to evoke past glories in service of hopeful new ones. San Francisco's Columbia Theatre was an early West Coast date for *The Broadway Melody*, ad encouragement to "bring the children" justified in part by added attraction of Laurel and Hardy in their first talking comedy, *Unaccustomed As We Are*, not ad-specified beyond the Columbia's mention of "good comedy" in support of *The Broadway Melody*.

↑

Gold Diggers of Broadway (1929)

But for a single column, this was an entire page that greeted Cleveland news readers in October 1929. *Gold Diggers of Broadway* was Warner Bros. pushing outer limit of musical extravagance. Might this be the one that finally exhausted a public with all singing and dancing? There is 100 percent color throughout, its "life-likeness" debatable, as Technicolor was then a limited two-tone process, with only red and green registering fully. It was by then common to compare local prices with higher rates demanded of New York patronage. In this case, *Gold Diggers* had played Gotham's Winter Garden at $2, well above what Hippodrome customers would be asked to pay. Again there is an ad-depicted chorus line to suggest music and spectacle, but these were not the novelty of six months earlier, and months made an enormous difference in terms of box-office response to talkies. We can evaluate Hippodrome selling with this ad, but no longer *Gold Diggers of Broadway*—it's a lost film but for fragments that have turned up since 1929.

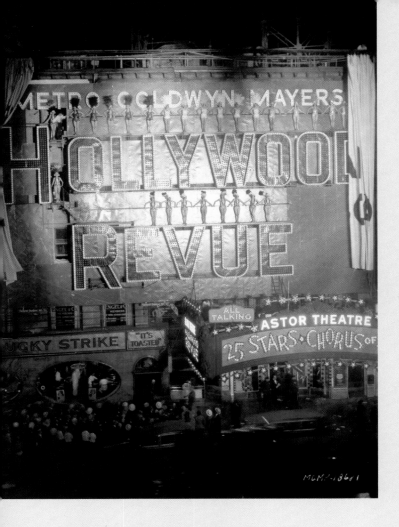

Broadway 1929

The big broom that was talkies swept away all of silence, a point well made by this August 1929 glimpse of crowded Broadway at the filmic fork of a Great White Way pointing in sound's direction. Mute drama was passé. The future belonged to *The Hollywood Revue of 1929* and big noises like it. The very title announced a takeover. MGM's rollout of stars in sound demanded not a mere billboard, but one festooned with chorus girls standing among electric bulbs and high above jammed streets. One Astor ad was as much about this display as a screen attraction that virtually sold itself. Was their sign the biggest of its sort in the world? To look upon the shower of light and scant-clad models would remove most doubt, if indeed there was any. Critics were at least fooled, or in Astor parlance, persuaded. *The Hollywood Revue of 1929* doesn't entertain a 21st century so much, but look at that mob wanting in. Yes, what they say about the past being a foreign country *has* got truth in it.

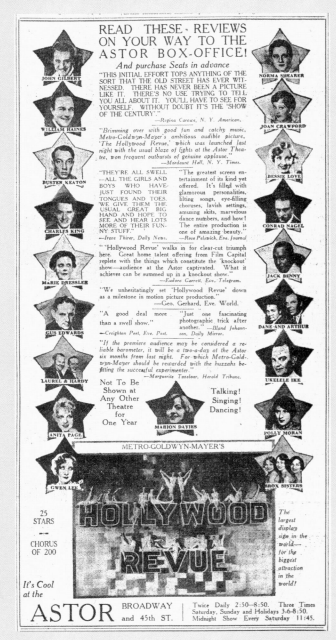

Two holdouts from *The Hollywood Revue of 1929* were Greta Garbo and Lon Chaney. Her talkie debut would be saved until a following year, and his MGM contract made speech a separately negotiable item. Result was both Garbo and Chaney in silent dramas as Metro colleagues spoke. *Thunder* was railroad action with the company's most popular player (hands down Chaney) using his accustomed pantomime to put points across. This show would be no slouch even in silence. All the Capitol needed was an ad glimpse of Chaney to fill seats, and hang whether or not he'd talk. A distinction the theatre had was its crowded stage show, a "Revue" that wasn't canned like what the Astor was offering. This meant plenty to those who preferred at least some of entertainment live, it being unlikely that disc-sound or Movietone could surpass emerging star Kate Smith in full and onstage voice.

Farther down Broadway, director John Ford, respected then, revered now, had his first talking feature, *The Black Watch,* opening at the Gaiety. This was from Fox Movietone, which meant a sound track on film rather than synchronized disc. We'd assume that to be a better process, but Movietone had issues too. Nobody's system was glitch-free. The Gaiety's added attraction of a sound newsreel was meaningful, however, Fox having made these a rage since scooping a show world with sound shots of the Lindbergh takeoff, which were shown but hours after that historic event. Here was where Movietone News made its reputation and capacity from there onward to draw customers. Gaiety bonus of Sherlock Holmes author Sir Arthur Conan Doyle in a spoken greet to the audience was all the more reason to attend *The Black Watch*, which could be safely sold as the "Most Thrilling All-Talking Production on Broadway," being there was less to compete with in a market still trying to dispose of silents in distribution pipelines.

↑

Animal Crackers (1930)

By 1930 musicals had worn their welcome to a point where advertising would all but conceal song/dance content. It was comedy now that sold the show, "Old Man Gloom" of a new-arrived Depression being put to rout by the merry Marxes and their anarchic upturn of convention. The "roaring Big Bertha of Mirth" was pre-sold from a year's run on Broadway, the Marx Bros. having proved themselves sufficiently as screen lure to become focal point for the Rex Theatre's ad. Was it the comedy team or Broadway origin of *Animal Crackers* that commended it to filmgoers? The Rex is reliant upon both for its campaign, along with a nod to itself as "home of the best sound in town."

→

General Crack (1930)

John Barrymore had been popular in silents, but this actor sans voice was like toast without jam. Fan base panted to hear him speak, and so came Vitaphone, first with Barrymore doing a Shakespeare excerpt for an all-star revue, *The Show of Shows*, then in 100 percent chat capacity for *General Crack*. "Cyclonic romance and adventure" is pledged by the Palace Theatre of Cincinnati—no need for modesty here, previous *Don Juan* and *The Sea Beast* having been "just shadows" of Barrymore's "vivid Vitaphone self." The Palace cunningly displays the famed Barrymore profile in both light and shadow, along with three separate images of the Great Lover in feminine embrace. Where this sort of attraction was concerned, no prose could be too purple; the "pent-up power" of his voice would make Barrymore seem a "living presence" as opposed to mute figure of yore. Cincinnati readers could hardly fail to be impressed—the Palace's ad for *General Crack* took up an entire newspaper page.

←

Anna Christie (1930)

A highest-profile holdout from talk was Greta Garbo. She'd succumb in 1930 with this carefully prepared vehicle to showcase her distinctive, if accented, voice. *Anna Christie* wisely cast Swedish-born Garbo in a Swedish role. Her voice in that event would not disappoint, the public hearing Garbo on the same terms as they'd been seeing her. Star voices needed to match pre-existing images. Staring-at-us art of Garbo in an ad otherwise given to copy and generous white space was effective convey of Garbo as centerpiece of the program, no matter the value of a "colossal stage show." Loew's Midland's phrase, "Greta Garbo Talks," would itself become famous, inspiring a 1984 film, *Garbo Talks*.

↑

The Rogue Song at the Astor (1930)

↑

The Rogue Song (1930)

"Not since Jenny Lind . . .," said premiere ads for Lawrence Tibbett and *The Rogue Song*, his a first operatic voice to star in talkies. Clearly for highbrows, but MGM hedged bets by casting Laurel and Hardy as comic sidekicks for the booming baritone. *The Rogue Song* was an ideal attraction to fill Broadway's Astor Theatre, an oasis of prestige where formal openings, as in full dress of patronage, came not as surprise on an opening night. The event wouldn't "revolutionize amusement history," though some may have been amused, if not annoyed, by the tendency of Tibbett's voice to blow out the Astor's sound system, an occurrence noted by post-premiere critics. This was a roadshow, $2 tops to get in, with seats sold up to four weeks in advance. The ad lends majesty via surround of Tibbett by lightning bolts, but didn't that merely confirm *The Rogue Song* as "canned" operetta as opposed to the real thing?

Loew's Midland, well named for its location in Kansas City, was owned by the parent company of MGM and took *The Rogue Song* in the wake (by months) of touted triumph on both coasts. Tibbett came, sang, but could he and *The Rogue Song* conquer KC? There'd be no tuxedos in evidence for this opening, and Laurel/Hardy ad depiction plus five acts of vaudeville would lighten load of perceived high art. Endorsement from stars better known than Lawrence Tibbett were added balm: Ramon Novarro, Joan Crawford, Lon Chaney, William Haines, Buster Keaton. All were MGM contract players obliged to help out, and maybe by the Midland's run, *The Rogue Song* needed all the help it could get. The headline "Electrifying!" points out mechanical reproduction of voices in the same way as the Astor ad's lightning bolts. Were these disclaimers—or a free use of superlatives that had an unintended consequence?

The Unholy Three (1930)

Two of the voices spoken by Lon Chaney in *The Unholy Three* are pictured on this Loew's Midland ad, the actor's own and one he'll undoubtedly instill in the sinister looking dummy on his lap. Such was the basis of Chaney appeal—"amazingly thrilling" with always a touch of the bizarre, if not horrific. Loew's emphasizes the voice to feed public assumption that Lon will match his thousand faces with as many variants of talk. *The Unholy Three* was sold everywhere on just such premise, it being natural that Chaney inflection went beyond the capacity of other players speaking. He was, after all, the Miracle Man of movies. The actor would sign an affidavit to effect that all of voices he'd use in *The Unholy Three* were his own. What more valuable publicity for a major name making a sound debut? For "laughs," there was Charlie Chase in *Fast Work*, the Loew's Midland knowing perhaps that Lon in five voices would leave patronage wrung out. Sad was the fact this would be Chaney's last. He had mastered sound, but would depart the mortal stage shortly after release of *The Unholy Three*.

City Lights (1931)

Q: What major star resisted talkies the longest?
A: Charlie Chaplin, because he could afford to. Chaplin made films with his own money, and that gave his Tramp protection against onslaught of talk that was ruination of clown colleagues hard put to match images with a voice. Chaplin took his time with *City Lights* and gambled that the public would accept universal language as silently conveyed by the Tramp since 1914. Philadelphia's Erlanger Theatre had an eye-catcher ad that promised free transport to *City Lights* via chartered (and double-decker) bus with appropriate banner. Here was rolling promotion and instrument of goodwill to spread word of a silent show that everyone in 1931 Philly should see. Integration of the bus into ads would alert readers not only to "ride free" advantage, but also specialness of *City Lights*. Result: "Knockout" ticket sales at the Erlanger and Chaplin staying for most of spring and summer seasons.

Socked by a Depression

It took a while for movies to feel the impact from the Great Depression. Continued interest in the revolution that was talkies made 1930 a good year at box offices. Industry cheerleaders would even characterize the biz as "Depression-proof," this before the fullest effect of the Crash was felt and coin spent for films had to be kept instead for essentials. The bite wiser heads saw coming was dug deep by 1931 and held a grip for uncomfortable seasons to follow. Several of the big studios went into bankruptcy or receivership, and theatres that had been built and bought so extravagantly now weighed like anchors upon ownership no longer able to carry debt on increasingly empty houses.

Attendance dropped sharply and some theatres closed or were sold. Others retrenched or tried new devices to lure patronage. Double features fooled folks into thinking they'd got more for admission money, plus there were gifts or prizes to bribe them into coming. Advertising had to make a better argument for admission harder got. Sex and scares would appeal to baser instinct, so ads got bluer and publishers more regulatory in wake of civic/parental complaint. A title assigned to D.W. Griffith's final feature in 1931, *The Struggle*, aptly described life among showmen through these leanest of years.

We know *All Quiet on the Western Front* as font of early talking prestige and an Academy winner for Best Picture. How then to reconcile that with such lurid selling as here? Desperation comes to mind—maybe Kansas City's Schubert Theatre was feeling pinch from the Crash. Theirs was a roadshow engagement, two-a-day with advanced admissions and seats reserved. The title is boldly presented, a center "sun" exuding rays toward the book from which Universal's film was adapted, along with a dressed-down flapper to represent French temptation. Were ad readers as tempted to see *All Quiet*? The "2nd Big Week" is, if anything, more direct. Smart showmen knew better than to sell *All Quiet on the Western Front* as grim war, even if its content was inarguably that. This was not grand spectacle after earlier fashion of *Wings* or the same year's *Hell's Angels*. The Schubert, knowing its marketplace, would lure patronage with sex, then let them realize on watching what a masterpiece *All Quiet* was.

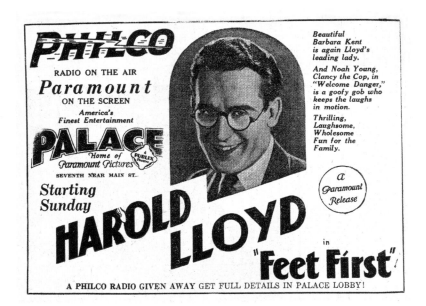

←

Feet First (1930)

Harold Lloyd was another who'd slip with the Depression, his go-getter lost in a landscape where so little could be got. The Fort Worth Palace's run of *Feet First* was less about Lloyd than a tie-up between that theatre and Philco, one of their radios to be given away during the film's engagement. This was not unlike inviting a fox to your henhouse, as what was radio but reason for folks to stay home and be amused? Philco sold more sets than any other maker, their cathedral-shaped wooden radio called a "Baby Grand" for its decorative splendor. Once in receipt of this, why go out to movies? And yet here was the unholy bargain theatres were obliged to make. Only one in an audience could win the prize, and others would presumably be back next time something was given away.

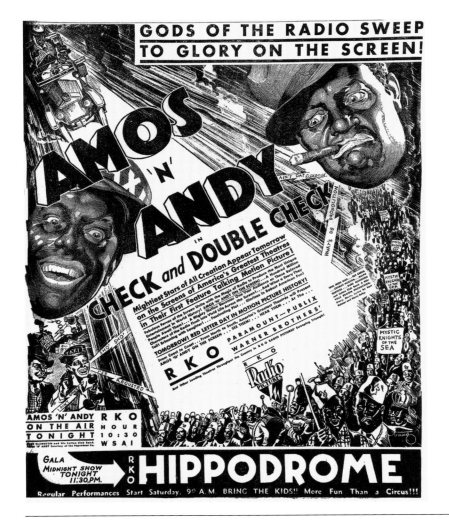

←

Check and Double Check (1930)

It was no hyperbole labeling Amos 'n' Andy "Gods of the Radio," merely statement of fact. The two did blackface minus cork on weekly airwave basis and kept people home so as not to miss their comedy broadcast. This, of course, was bane of theatres left empty thanks to A 'n' A scooping up trade. What to do about rival radio except to embrace it? Newly formed RKO Radio Pictures, note the middle name, was offspring of media giant RCA, the latter with its own sound process and eagerness to exploit that plus interests in wireless amusement. To wed film with radio's largest lure was a path to enormous profit for RKO, *Check and Double Check* meriting full-page ad treatment when it opened at Cleveland's Hippodrome Theatre, former vaudeville address and lately acquired by RKO. We recall little of Amos 'n' Andy today, and less of *Check and Double Check*, but it and they were mortgage lifters for embattled theatres that fairly fought to play a first screen translation of radio's most popular act.

How to Sell an Outmoded Product, Times Three

Clara Bow had been making whoopee for Paramount since the mid-'20s, the "It" girl when "it" was a carefree Jazz Age fueled by gravy off rising stocks. Promoting Bow seemed as simple as the plug-in of a vacuum cleaner that sucked up cash. Her initial talkie, *The Wild Party*, had drawn ducats for curiosity, now satisfied. That she was stifled by sound was apparent in Bow's voice as well as inaction. There'd be no bounce off soundstage walls, what with microphones dogging her every move. Who needed flappers anyhow, once the bottom fell out? Well, Paramount and affiliated theatres, topping a thousand just in ones they owned, certainly would need Bow and profits she once guaranteed. Trouble was, they'd lessen, greased by a just-crashed stock market (*The Saturday Night Kid* released during fateful 10/29), this on the eve of the talkie-driven move toward players who could better portray a changed world's reality.

Paramount and the Colonial Theatre would tout *The Saturday Night Kid* as their "All-Talking New Show World Picture," a mouthful to make us ask just what a "new show world" might amount to. It wasn't sound—that thrill was going, if not gone. Patronage had heard screens talk and were ready for movies to start moving again. Clara Bow, even if "cuter than ever," would find her "little go-getter" at impasse insofar as public reception of more of the same. These ads, however, represent the summit of home office skill, the Colonial having taken receipt of work prepared by Paramount artists and transferring it more or less intact to newspaper pages. Such elegance and persuasion, run over a three-day period in Philadelphia, illustrate grasp of product by Paramount and its east coast sales division. Company layout and copy came to fullest flowering even as their subject was beginning her decline.

Let's Go!

VACATIONS are over. Brisk Fall days are here! We can't blame things on the weather any longer. The United States, as rich, bountiful and fundamentally sound as ever has been marking time. It's time we made things happen.

Think of 122,000,000 people in the United States with needs to be satisfied, desires to be fulfilled, dreams to be realized. *Let's go!* Let's celebrate Prosperity Week right now. Idle money will retard prosperity more than idle hands. Buy now. Prices are lower, values are greater today than they have been in years. You hire people, you start factories, you keep the wheels turning, you help yourself when you buy something and you *get what you want* with it all.

Get plenty of wholesome entertainment, too. It's a fundamental need — the difference between monotony and satisfaction in life. *There's* one dollar as big as a rainbow today and there are many others just as big. Motion

Pictures were never better or bigger bargains than they are today. *Let's go!*

In 1930, Paramount Publix Corporation, leaders in motion pictures, offers the most ambitious production program in its history. With studios in Hollywood and New York operating at capacity. With its largest roster of stars. An army of **directors**, authors, showmen.

This program of **Paramount's** Greater New Show World is climaxed in October, November and December with mighty **Paramount** Pictures that will **make** every family in the **land** talk and TALK. **Beginning** with the release for Prosperity Week, October 5th to 11th, of the romantic comedy hit "Monte Carlo" followed by an unbroken series of superproductions. *Let's go!*

Let's Go!

ERNST LUBITSCH'S
"MONTE CARLO"
with
JACK BUCHANAN and
JEANETTE MacDONALD

CHARLES ROGERS
in "Heads Up"
with Victor Moore, Helen Kane

NANCY CARROLL
in "Laughter"
with Fredric March, Frank Morgan

JACK OAKIE
in "Sea Legs"

"If it's a Paramount Picture, it's the best show in town!"

Paramount [logo] **Pictures**

PARAMOUNT PUBLIX CORPORATION, ADOLPH ZUKOR, PRES.   PARAMOUNT BUILDING, NEW YORK

← Let's Go, Paramount (1931)

It was over a year since the Crash. 1931's horizon was showing clouds for a lucky-till-now picture industry. How to keep people attending theatres even as stomachs went empty? Solution: Instill optimism. Prosperity wasn't just around the corner, said this Paramount institutional ad—it was already here. The enemy was "idle money," that is, money not deposited at box offices. There was no "bigger or better bargain" than motion pictures, which was sort of true when compared with legit or what was left of vaudeville, but a deeper probe would reveal radio as a truest value. It was, after all, free once you bought the set. Still, ads like this were game effort on at least one company's part to sustain moviegoing habits in the face of economic crisis. That Paramount would, in March 1933, face its own crisis of receivership, was an irony not lost on industry observers.

← The Struggle (1931)

Here is further refutation of a Jazz Age distinctly passed. No longer are such excesses celebrated, *The Struggle* positing a "wilderness of pleasure" as harbinger for disaster that followed. D.W. Griffith's final film dealt with alcoholism, a hangover, said many, from the '20s. Such brutal scars were salt to wounds from a deepening Depression. Was it a wonder that *The Struggle* flopped? And yet, here were ads prepared by the Pantages Theatre in Kansas City to expertly depict the duel of drink/debauch with home and hearth, a "strong, sturdy, stalwart" man who is "ambushed by temptation." Straight-up exploitation films actually did this sort of thing better—or at least to a public's greater satisfaction. Griffith was perhaps too earnest in his condemnation, taking all of fun out of spiral-downs. We could wonder if sleaze merchants later "borrowed" some of Pantages' striking art for *The Struggle* to dress up ads for their own treatments of "realism on a rampage."

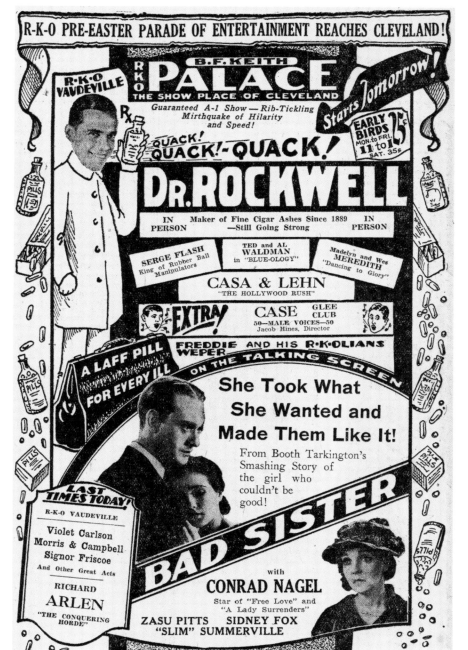

Laughing one's way out of hard times was at least temporary balm for what ailed audiences and theatres increasingly desperate to attract them. Cleveland's prescription at the RKO Palace was filled by live-appearing Dr. (Quack, Quack, Quack) Rockwell, "Maker of Fine Cigar Ashes Since 1889." We may safely assume from all this that senses of humor found differing levels in 1931, and who knows but what a quack, quack "Mirthquake" might prove to be just that where 3,284 seats are filled and hungering for laughter's relief. Dr. Rockwell was a stalwart of vaudeville and played New York's fabled Palace, so would be known and welcomed by Clevelanders. Of Serge Flash, "King of Rubber Ball Manipulators," there is less known. All this and the 50-voice Case Glee Club, plus the seeming afterthought of feature attraction *Bad Sister*, bode well for a matinee's quarter admission, and yet— consider the groceries and home heating 25 cents might contribute toward in 1931. Priorities had to be weighed carefully before *any* entertainment outing.

↑

Cimarron (1931)

An epic perhaps too mighty for its own good, *Cimarron* lost money for RKO despite winning Best Picture for 1932. Was empire building regarded too much a pipe dream for Depression dwellers? Anyway, those who came were impressed. The real problem for RKO was the excess they spent to produce the thing. Prestige counted for something, however, and *Cimarron* had that in spades. This was a picture you could lay down red carpet for, as evidenced by gala that attended Cincinnati's world premiere at the RKO Palace. *Cimarron* would be an event they'd let schools out for, celebrations begun early and sometimes lasting days. Here too was where radio could serve theatre rivals, with live broadcasting from the Palace's crowded lobby. If *Cimarron* wasn't altogether a "Flame-Shot Meteor Swirling to Earth," it could stand abreast with mighty forebears *The Birth of a Nation* and *The Four Horsemen of the Apocalypse*, two with which it shared epic stature.

↑
The Guilty Generation (1931) and Flesh/Robber's Roost (1932)

Double features as avenue out of the Depression: would two for one bring back a retreating audience? Similar marketing worked in other fields of retail. More-for-your-money was a concept anyone could understand. Ads promising a pair of "First-Run Hit Pictures" made crowds feel they'd gotten in twice on a single admission. Distributors took the hit for rentals cleaved by half, film companies economizing on features they knew would play second on theatre bills. Result: the "B" movie as part of major studio policy. The Kansas City Pantages conveys 1931 richness of its steepled front if not wealth of entertainment inside, *The Guilty Generation* and *The Bargain* being programmers by any measure. A "programmer" was what its name implied, just another block among shorts, a cartoon, newsreel, or a second feature. The Pantages offers at least spirited selling, the accusing finger pointing from upper left into the ad, with characters looking from the right with alarm. Whoever laid this one out knew his drama, and readership.

Loew's State led with its chin, stating outright and boldly that theirs was "The Greatest Amusement Value in America!" which may have been accurate enough were it not for thousands of other theatres offering similar value by 1932. It was important to emphasize that both features were "From the World's Greatest Producers," this to quell concern that one good show was being swapped for a pair of duds. Thus two major studios are specifically mentioned—Metro-Goldwyn-Mayer and Fox. A newsreel and Flip the Frog cartoon swelled Loew's program to three hours, which made for less audience turnover, this plus low admissions (15 cents for matinees, children a dime at all times) must have made break-even seem a distant goal.

I Am a Fugitive from a Chain Gang (1932)

First, the title. Everyone knew of chain gangs and abuses attendant on them. Such was regarded a Southern problem, thus ease and comfort of pile-on for watchers located elsewhere. Warner Bros. made *I Am a Fugitive*, with muckraking from there the joy of ad artists who seldom had such red meat to chew on. Multiple samplings are here to illustrate myriad ways a 1932–33 public could be lit up. Who was ready for 90 minutes of modern-set cruelty and debasement? Everyone, it seemed, for *I Am a Fugitive* earned some of WB's best profit for that year. The "True!" aspect burned bright-est, and yes, this *had* been a modern crucifixion by many a believable account. They say the movie brought about reforms, though I wonder if it was actually ads like these that lowered booms.

Fugitive's author being still on the run even as the picture played first-runs was ambrosia to selling, and keynote to those ads that proved most effective. Positive reviews wouldn't confuse *I Am a Fugitive* with low-down exploitation its selling evoked, so you'd not feel besmirched for going. To see this, in fact, was fulfillment of civic responsibility. There was day-to-day suspense as to whether real-life subject Robert Elliot Burns (renamed James Allen for the film) would be caught, making *I Am a Fugitive* truly a show to promote alongside headlines. Up-to-minute impact was further emphasized by November 1932 election returns broadcast to Warner's Lake patronage "via Western Union wire" on world premiere night in Cleveland.

An interesting adjunct to ads for *I Am a Fugitive* was this contest running in support of the (Fort) Worth Theatre's opening. Planted "reviews," personality profiles, and movie-based puzzles were common to Amusement Pages. This one challenges readers to locate fugitive Paul Muni amidst the swamp, with free Worth tickets to the first 10 winners. Can *you* spot him?

Find the Fugitive From a Chain Gang Here!

Somewhere, hidden in this swamp, is Paul Muni, playing the role of James Allen, the fugitive in I Am a Fugitive From a Chain Gang, new film opening Friday at the Worth. Can you find him? A pair of guest tickets to see the picture will go to each of the first 10 persons who draw a ring around Muni and send the clipped drawing to the Movie Editor of The Press. Go!

↑
Hold 'Em Jail (1932)

↑
She Done Him Wrong (1932)

Theatres during the Depression were very much about offering more for limited money, showmen eager to contrast plenty on their inside with austerity in the streets. Moviegoing needed to be an escape as never before. A loaded bill, with accent on comedy, made for "greater shows" well beyond what was offered on the screen. What was left of vaudeville saw extended life in picture houses, especially where lean times meant shopping for entertainment's best value. The RKO Mainstreet uses a tower of smiling faces to promote its "Show of Shows That Comes Once in a Lifetime!" or at least until the bill changes the following week.

As to further heat-seeking, there came in 1932 what would be Paramount's temporary salvation in the person of Mae West, a sex siren to rout the blues from box offices nationwide before censorship sent her bawdy act packing. *She Done Him Wrong* was a first for West in star capacity, stage reputation and sizzling support to George Raft in *Night After Night* having preceded. The Shea's mention of *Sex* and *Diamond Lil* was reference to "positive sensation" these had been on Gotham stages. Broadway counted for plenty when it bore fruit of personalities later co-opted by Hollywood. A "hot time" for Buffalo was further assured by bonus performance of legit hit *Whoopee*, being done complete at Shea's as opposed to a tab (that is, short or "tabloid") version, normally the resort of film houses using plays as support for screen fare. Note attention grab of hand-writ Mae West and feature title. Was this to simulate graffiti used in less polite places to announce Mae and *She Done Him Wrong*?

←

Blood Money (1933)
The Rider of Death Valley (1932)

Speaking of free rides, or waltzes, here is less tangible gift-giving by Schine's Hi-Art Theatre, where kids attending a double-bill of *Blood Money* and Tim McCoy in *Man of Action* (plus a serial chapter—whew!) also get an hour's free dance lesson conducted onstage by presumed local "Miss Tessie." Such deportment in youth was encouraged by genteel parents then, so porridge of entertainment like this was not unusual by standard and habits of 1933. We might inquire as to ratio of boys vis-à-vis girls with regard the dance lessons. Would this come before or after seeing Tim McCoy slap leather and whoop-up on bad guys? The Hi-Art breaks layout rules in a crowded and somewhat confused bill of fare, especially as this was mere two-column advertising of minimal depth. Programs were jamming up as customers demanded more for their change, this a boon for bargain seekers, if a puzzle for ad readers.

More to liking of boys would have been giveaway of a "live pony" (one would hope they'd not give away a dead one). And what better screen companion for the drawing than Tom Mix in his talking western, *The Rider of Death Valley*? Youngsters surely felt it worth the gamble of a quarter to possibly win a "beauiful" mount (spelling errors not uncommon to ads, then or now). Issue arising is how parents of the sudden steed owner would react when Junior's prize was brought home to feed and curry. Schine's Palace had 1,100 seats and was located in Lockport, New York. It was a small house by comparison with palaces seating several times as many patrons, but how many of them gave away ponies at a Saturday matinee?

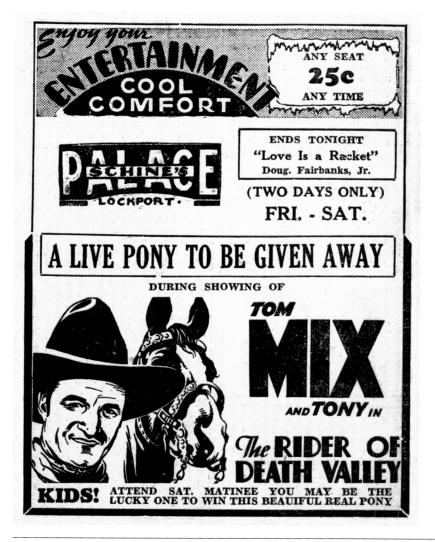

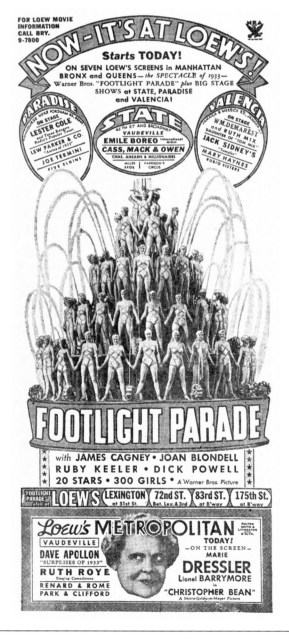

←

Gold Diggers of 1933 (1933)
Footlight Parade (1933)

Here was meeting of the humble and the grand, against backdrop of musicals that revived the genre during Depression years. Hoyt's was a 514-seat house in Fort Smith, Arkansas, probably lucky to get *Gold Diggers of 1933* at all, let alone on "sensational pre-release" basis (doubtful, as body of this ad was home office pre-prepared). Noteworthy is apparent lift of policy that let children in free to Hoyt's—for *Gold Diggers* they must occupy a paid seat thanks to "high cost of this picture" to the theatre. Manhattan, Bronx, and Queens was something else entirely, a first sub-run for follow-up *Footlight Parade* after a Broadway premiere stand. This saturation of palaces, each with thousands of seats, was where Warner Bros. got back lavish spending for their Busby Berkeley specials. The State, Paradise, and Valencia loaded up further with vaudeville, a minimum of four acts at each location. Did even thrift shoppers find this too much of a good thing?

→

Looking Forward (1933)

A primary goal for any layout artist was arresting copy, that which would stop a reader cold and cause him/her to study your ad in toto, and then proceed posthaste to topic attraction. Presidential endorsement of specific movies were/are rare. We could probably count them on a single hand. Imagine then, MGM and aligned theatres' excitement when Franklin Roosevelt lent chief executive hand to promotion of *Looking Forward*, a 1933 drama dealing with rise/fall against business backdrop with, naturally, an upbeat finish. "Then it was realized . . ." that the film's title was also that of Roosevelt's recently completed book, says the ad memo. Sure sounds like a fix—perhaps collusion between Metro and the White House to sell book and film? Anyway, *Looking Forward* benefited both, and word of FDR having seen and enjoyed the movie was wealth beyond measure for MGM's selling arm. I doubt we'd find first-run ads for *Looking Forward* that didn't center such a once-in-a-blue-moon co-op.

→

King Kong (1933)

King Kong is one Depression-era monument that still stands, having been remade twice (more if we count variants and a meeting with Godzilla). One could ruminate as to Kong representing the Crash and hard times, but let's not. Focus might better be upon New York's ad splash for dual opening at lush-beyond-words Radio City Music Hall and its but slightly less ornate companion, the RKO Roxy. Combined seating of these would hopefully be enough to contain mobs who'd damn the Depression and spend dollars for Gotham's absolute must-see. *Kong* was mightiest on the East Coast, his reach not so long in the west, but then they didn't have a brand-new Empire State Building as focal point to selling. What was more surefire than your giant gorilla atop a tallest skyscraper located mere blocks away? New Yorkers wouldn't miss *King Kong*, the one circus they'd willingly swap bread for.

It Happened One Night (1934)

Whatever prosperity was just around corners
came in form of theatres playing *It Happened
One Night*, a legendary hit and trendsetter
that pitted romantic comedy against harsh-
est backdrop of Depression-era life on the
road. Maybe 1934 was time to lighten up and
laugh a bit at hardship, though likelier was
timing (perfect) and star combination plus
a director in Frank Capra who understood
mood of the moment. "Wham" as exclaimed
by Cleveland's Circle Theatre was apt, and
they weren't hyperbolizing those thousands
who wanted to see *It Happened One Night*,
or see it again. Wham with a wake that
forms an arrow pointing downward to the
theatre name was ad invention that drew
plaudits from trade brethren who'd borrow
the device themselves where occasion called.
It Happened One Night had, by then, taken
its sweep of Academy Awards, while repeat
business, as suggested by the ad, was seeing encore bookings pay off like first-runs.
Many a showman would recall *It Happened
One Night* as white light and salvation
during hard-tack Depression years.

Pen and Ink Said It Best

There were but two colors a newspaper could effectively reproduce in gone days, but infinite variation on each. Black and white was finessed as skillfully in ads as in movies shot on monochrome. Strongest of impression could be made by pen-and-ink art because this tended to reproduce well, even on daily sheets. There was detail lost, yes, and we can but imagine what original boards, as submitted by artists, would look like. Much pen-and-ink work was signed, at least with an initial if not a name. Future Disney animator Milt Kahl toiled at Fox West Coast easels during the early '30s, as did notable others who began careers doing ad layout.

Pen and ink put depth and dimension to imagery that flattered both star and dramatic situation. Multiple layers of ink lent texture way past capacity of reproduced photos, which tended not to register well in newspapers. Large circuits kept staff who were oft-times trained artists, from which a number would transition to fine art and painting later. Ad work generated on circuit easels would fan out to member theatres and be entirely different from more conventional art in pressbooks. Pen and ink was close work, never done in a rush. Instruments used looked like a dentist's drill set. Variety of ways to lay down ink included the row of lines called hatching, which when crisscrossed became cross-hatching. There was contour-hatching, which followed the curve or outline of a subject, while scumbling and stippling used tiny, squiggly circular lines or plethora of small dots, respectively, to provide atmosphere or shading. Pen and ink combined these techniques to render much of what was best in theatre ads, especially during the late '20s and the early '30s when the format was at a peak of use.

↑
Intolerance (1916)

An early example of pen and ink put to task of showmanship was D.W. Griffith's massive 1916 follow-up to *The Birth of a Nation*.

↑
The Trial of Mary Dugan (1929)

On-trial Norma Shearer looks properly distraught, if not dissipated, thanks to ink application around her startled eyes.

↓

The Pagan (1929)

Solids in hair and rich detail of the lead lady's sarong is set off by stippling and broken-line background.

↓

The Blue Angel (1929/1930)

That dangerous stare of Marlene Dietrich beckons us enter sordid environ of *The Blue Angel*, German-made in 1929, U.S. released in 1930.

↑

Mothers Cry (1930)

The home office may have cried for this ad's violation of cardinal ad rules: Never have your figure staring out of the border, lest reader's eye follow.

←

Morocco (1930)

Dietrich again, in what was actually the first of her vehicles released in America, and note the star's pale expression in contrast to dark and aggressive lead man Gary Cooper.

↑
Charley's Aunt (1930)

The artist here puts over the fact that it's funnyman Charlie Ruggles behind femme attire of the title character, one well known to legit-goers for years before this first talkie version of *Charley's Aunt* arrived in 1930.

↗
Lightnin' (1930)

No ad exaggerated when calling Will Rogers "America's wit," and no image spoke plainer to plain folks than man-of-the-people Will, art of him alone sufficient to fill seats during bleak years of Depression.

→
Billy the Kid (1930)

John Mack Brown's Billy looks one way at sheriff Wallace Beery and gallops another in a socko ad that's got action coming and going.

↑
The Lash (1931)

A dense-lined backdrop sets off romantic art of Richard Barthelmess as a "debonair desperado" of the plains.

↑
No Limit (1931)

Pen-and-ink legend Milt Kahl initialed this strong combo of playing cards and saucy Clara Bow to emphasize *No Limit*'s gambling theme.

←

The Criminal Code (1931)

Background of bars and a forgotten prisoner heightens effect of this ad for director Howard Hawks' look-in at prison conditions.

→

Scandal Sheet (1931)

Ruthless editor George Bancroft phones in dirt as faithless wife Kay Francis seeks embrace of Clive Brook.

←

Reducing (1931)

What better to capture comedic expression than pen and ink, as here utilized on behalf of popular duo Marie Dressler and Polly Moran in one of their MGM howlers.

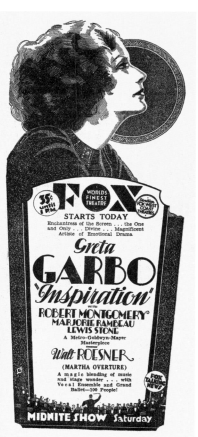

→

Inspiration (1931)

Garbo in profile, or otherwise, was a natural for selling, and here she's posed against a cameo that sets off distinct features of the Swedish Sphinx.

→

Cleopatra (1934)

Wonderful pen-ink evocation of dramatic elements put to work by Cecil B. DeMille for his 1934 spectacular.

Wonders That Dazzle The Human Imagination!

Cleopatra's Paradise, a Love Boat 500 feet long, where Antony is wafted to unknown delights by the sloe-eyed Temptress of Egypt!

Galaxies of Roman beauties bathing in rose-scented palace pools, laughing over the latest scandal with Roman court dandies!

Giant War Galleys hurling fire balls, armies of men in holocaust of battle, all for a woman's love!

The Ballet of the sinuous "Leopards", the Dance on the back of the Sacred Bull, performed by the 100 sea-maidens!

Rome's conquering hordes shocked into silence by what they see in the crimson-columned throne room at Alexandria!

The rites to Isis, Goddess of Love, into whose worship Antony is initiated by the singing handmaidens!

Cleopatra borne in Caesar's triumph, dazzling the Roman multitudes, decked in priceless gold and jewels, as the Great White Queen of Egypt!

The last exquisite love tryst of Antony and Cleopatra, the weeping slave sent for the fatal stinging asp! "I am dying, Egypt, dying but the world is well lost for love!"

•

A Paramount Picture

A Love Affair That Shook The World...And Toppled Two Empires!

CLEOPATRA

Cecil B. DeMille's tremendous pageant of unrivaled splendor!

with

CLAUDETTE COLBERT

Warren **WILLIAMS**

Henry **WILCOXON**

Ian Keith   Joseph Schildkraut

and

Thousands of Others!

STARTS TOMORROW!   R K O   **ALBEE**

Ads Strip Bare to Heat Up Attendance

Pre-Code has been studied much of late. There really was no such term during the period it flourished. Essence of the Production Code was rules the screen had to follow with regard to content of movies, idea being to minimize sex, violence, endorsement of low morality—in other words, what much of human conduct was about. Rawer meat had a way of rousing curiosity, if not baser emotion, and so producers, later abetted by advertising, fed appetites of young and old who liked being treated as adults. Pre-Code as currently defined ran from early talkies to summer of 1934 when the film industry submitted to strict enforcement of a Production Code that had been there all along, if observed less strenuously.

Many ads went further than films they promoted. As Hollywood ducked the censor, so too would theatres play tag with newspaper editors who'd cry foul over art or copy or both that violated community standard. Children looking at the family paper were naturally lured by graphic display on Amusement Pages, especially when, by parent standards, it got *too* graphic. Complaints could spell hazard to everyone's paycheck, black tar stuck to reputations of both the newspaper and theatres advertising with it. Larger circuits constantly warned management against "unclean" promotion, but showmen knew their customers sought heat whatever the season, so onward came ads that tickled boundaries.

Hot for Paris (1929)

The underdressed siren sitting atop a thermometer to yell "Get Hot!" sums up all that was pre-Code, even if the term itself was then unknown. Mason City, Iowa's Cecil Theatre ran these three ads over as many days to let corn-belters know there was something Hot, Hot, Hot going on inside. Bursting mercury brought on by repeat disrobing were motifs the Cecil would drum into promotion and sensibility of Amusement Page lookers. Especially creative was the Cecil's morning-after cartooned impression of a Saturday opening. Who'd resist the "sizzling furnace of fun" after peek at this?

↑
The Divorcée (1930)

Three that starred Norma Shearer would explain methods of modern love. She was the apostle of square deals for women in relation to men, an abolisher of double standards. It had begun as Shearer and MGM's effort to amend her image, *The Divorcée* a move toward sophisticated parts. Showmen seized initiative and ran ads positioning *The Divorcée* as mirror to a new morality. "Her sin was no greater than his—but she was a woman" took off on a hot issue and put fidelity, his *and* hers, on the griddle. Shearer with champagne and Chester Morris pointing finger of accusation made issues clear. Ads for *The Divorcée* unmasked "today's hot pursuit of pleasure" as prelude to breakup of homes; only this time, two would play at the game of straying.

↑

A Free Soul (1931)

Reuse of key art from *The Divorcée* tips off *A Free Soul* as more of same. Latter would re-plow fertile ground that was women's sexual emancipation, an issue Hollywood sought to address as had novels and stage plays before it. Ad makers saw exploitation value in a heroine who'd take care of herself "in your man's world." That would mean but one thing to readers, making ads simple to decode.

↑

Strangers May Kiss (1931)

The "free, white, and 21" adage was modified with insertion of "over" to acknowledge Norma Shearer's comparative maturity (she was 29). *Strangers May Kiss* was otherwise further meditation on the cost of free love. Pre-Code copy was very much about consequence of sexual license, soiled doves learning the hard way that "men may mix many things but they take their women STRAIGHT." The Shearer cycle couldn't have lasted, even with a continued lax Code—these films, and ads for them, having taken on decidedly uniform appearance.

→

Once a Sinner (1931)

Naughty step-ins to augment art, a title to sell itself ("Girl
with a past" copy seems, in fact, redundant), and that word
"daring," which Fox West Coast Theatres banned from ads,
but was it worse than copy they *did* use?

↓

Blonde Venus (1931)

"She liked variety," plus legs apart makes unmistakable the content of *Blonde Venus*, wherein Marlene Dietrich enlists in the Oldest
Profession, but for noblest of cause.

→

Safe in Hell (1931)

Her lips being "for many" was phrasing used often to sell pre-
Codes, as it could be plugged into virtually any of them, *Safe in
Hell* a standout for title and ad art getting straight to the point.

They called cooperation "voluntary," but exhibitors knew that to violate rules could mean expulsion from newsprint, shun by colleagues, and possibly an end of access to film product. "Lapse of good taste" by one advertiser translated to black eyes for all, wide elements of press or public at the ready to tar Hollywood with censorship's brush.

The self-regulatory Advertising Code had been instituted by the Motion Picture Association Of America in 1930, "little and infrequent cause for complaint over its record" since, said *Boxoffice* editor Ben Shlyen, who did acknowledge disregard of the Code by "lone wolf operators" from time to time, thus MPAA resolve in 1947 to again declare "ethical and moral responsibility" via revision of its Code to guide publicity and ad makers.

Representatives from all major film companies would "submit cheerfully" to tightened policy, while asserting their "freedom of decent expression," leaving courts of public opinion, and occasionally local lawmakers, to determine how much freedom their varying standards of decency might permit.

Mr. Exhibitor....

This is the Revised Motion Picture Advertising Code!

The revised advertising code of the Motion Picture Association of America provides a high standard of operation for exhibitors everywhere. Applying to all publicity, advertising and exploitation, it is wholly voluntary, but strict adherence to its provisions will further strengthen the theatre's position of responsibility within the community. As revised by the Association's Board of Directors, after careful consideration by the Advertising Advisory Council, composed of the directors of advertising and publicity of all major companies, the code outlines a specific course of action for all exhibitors. Avoid all censure and all censors! Abide by the code!

THE CODE

1 We subscribe to a code of business ethics based upon truth, honesty and integrity. All motion picture advertising shall
   (a) Conform to fact.
   (b) Scrupulously avoid all misrepresentation.

2 Good taste shall be the guiding rule of motion picture advertising.

3 Illustrations and text in advertising shall faithfully represent the pictures themselves.

4 No false or misleading statements shall be used directly, or implied by type arrangements or by distorted quotations.

5 No text or illustration shall ridicule or tend to ridicule any race, religion or religious faith; no illustration of a character in clerical garb shall be shown in any but a respectful manner.

6 The history, institutions and nationals of all countries shall be represented with fairness.

7 Profanity and vulgarity shall be avoided.

8 Pictorial and copy treatment of officers of the law shall not be of such a nature as to undermine their authority.

9 Specific details of crime, inciting imitation, shall not be used.

10 Motion picture advertisers shall be guided by the provision of the Production Code that the use of liquor in American life shall be restricted to the necessities of characterization and plot.

11 Nudity with meretricious purpose and salacious postures shall not be used; and clothed figures shall not be represented in such manner as to be offensive or contrary to good taste or morals.

12 Court actions relating to censoring of pictures, or other censorship disputes, are not to be capitalized in advertising or publicity.

Too Young to Marry (1931)

As revealing as wedding veils could be, theatres like the Strand weren't for decorum where it came to peek into bridal chamber that was *Too Young To Marry*. Would an ad like this lead to vows taken in near or altogether nudity?

The Hot Heiress (1931)

Watch that hand, mister! Well, maybe not, if he's the plumber she'll blister lips with. Ads like this cried for intervention—we can but be surprised it didn't come sooner.

↑
Young Sinners (1931)

What was 1931 youth if not in rebellion? The artist here conveys anything but disapproval of partiers "tramping on life" and enjoying the "cocktail" that was unbridled sin.

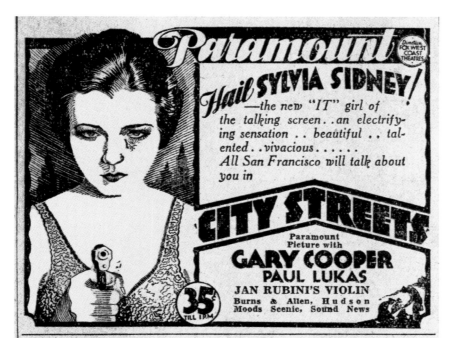

Red-Headed Woman (1932)

"Red" spelled in flame and a svelte Jean Harlow trade on notorious repute of a source novel that spelled out Standard Operating Procedure for home-wreckers, this ad and *Red-Headed Woman* being cheerful violations of a hobbled Production Code.

→

I'm No Angel (1933)

Indeed, "nothing else matters" but cash coming into theatres where Mae West played, her first two vehicles a bawdy sensation before censorship pulled teeth. "Just a gal who lost her reputation . . . but never missed it" was the San Francisco Embassy's thumbing of nose at the local restrictions *I'm No Angel* would undermine.

↓

She Had to Say Yes (1933)

No one asked, "Yes to what?" Ad readers were savvy to that affirmative as prelude to good girls going wrong.

↑
Hoopla (1933)

Clara Bow would be gone from movies after this one, but you'd not figure *Hoopla* for a swan song, what with more than 20 images of her incorporated into the Century's ad, leg art a focal point and nicely foregrounded from balance of art.

↑
Lilly Turner (1933)

It could be anyone standing there with legs bare and spread, but not Ruth Chatterton, whose image this clearly isn't, but what matter to Ambassador's artist, who knew "Too Much of a Woman" could be *any* woman where a single column was all you had to close the sale.

The Crash That Let Loose Monsters

Many have floated a link between the Depression and a vogue for horror films that began with *Dracula* in 1931, but what of Lon Chaney and fright he generated during the '20s? Maybe it was talking pictures rather than hard times that gave us appetite for all things terrifying. Sound was enhancement to horror, being a first occasion to hear things go bump in nights at the theatre. Known among showmen were monsters as readiest brand to promote, chillers a virtual synonym for exploitation. The genre went hand-in-hand with violence and sex, screen fiends disposed to kill and satisfy lusts minus protocol observed by mortal men. Desire was unleashed too among women, who'd pay to imagine themselves in a vampire's embrace or carried off by Frankenstein's monster. Submission to undead or unearthly things was very much a theme of advertising that could at times be more explicit than the films being promoted.

The gorge on horror was mostly spent by the mid-'30s, a combination of censorship and waning interest to blame for supernatural themes giving way to more earthbound topics. Peak of fascination, however, brought lines to thrillers that were less on-the-nose shock than Gothic romance, a sort not unlike literary tradition from which much of so-called horror derived. What this newest cycle did was take supernatural themes seriously, challenging us to accept undead bloodsuckers, raised corpses, and resurrected mummies as things within realm of possibility. Hadn't science come far enough, after all, to make a Frankenstein's creation plausible?

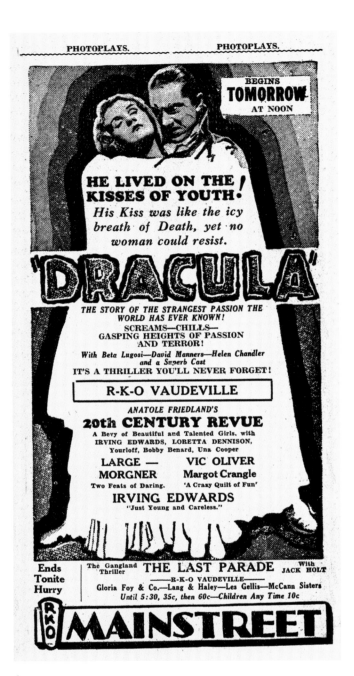

↑
Dracula (1931)

A "kiss that was like the icy breath of Death" would seem repugnant, but who knew how appetites ran among women and girls who made *Dracula* a towering sex symbol for 1931? This couldn't *all* have been a consequence of the Depression. Impulses were awakened that even ticket buyers were loath to ponder, lurid ads being, as usual, the alarm clock. "Gasping Heights of Passion and Terror" was something few films could boast, the vampire "no woman could resist" promising things unwholesome by measure of conventional leading men who'd offer much, but not eternal life as did Dracula.

↑
Frankenstein (1931)

There was tradition of a sort behind these new thrillers, as pointed up by the Warner Bros. Strand for its run of *Frankenstein*. Chaney-created monsters had gone before, and *Dracula* would serve as point of recent comparison. Screen fiends as "Immortal Characters" anticipates immortality conferred by generations to come who would embrace them in tribute magazines and late night TV, an eventuality this layout artist could hardly have seen coming. "To See It Is to Wear a Badge of Courage" was familiar device for selling horror movies that would follow for 50 years, the challenge to mostly youth who'd regard *Frankenstein* and others as gateway to maturity. Bragging rights for having got through these was at least as valued as marbles or money.

←

Doctor X (1932)

There was such thing as reflex copy where applied to certain sorts of product. For horror films, it was "Can You Take It," with or without a question or exclamation mark. In either case, a challenge to bravery of an audience, the "Badge of Courage" at stake again. Boys could impress dates by steeling it through a *Doctor X*, and chillers provoked more physical contact in seats, an outcome presumably sought by both sexes. *Doctor X* was among early rivals to the Universal brand, with addition of primitive Technicolor, actually more effective for being that, sickly hues ideal to put *X*'s thrills across.

←

White Zombie (1932)

United Artists really gave copyists one they could run with here. The title alone was ripest fruit for selling, a "zombie bride" wedded to sex aspect of ads. Near-nudity in art was invite to spectacle of souls (specifically women's) enslaved by hypnotic Bela Lugosi, whose best follow-up to *Dracula* this was. Beams from Lugosi eyes penetrate strategic points on the supine figure before him, a pushing-limits device that taken slightly further might have been nixed by the newspaper. Note too how one horror washes hands of another—among extras are screen tests for "Panther Woman" winners, this contest to find a leading actress for Paramount's upcoming shudder show, *Island of Lost Souls*.

↑

The Mummy (1932)

As 1932 drew toward close and chillers seemed less novel, the horror cycle's value as Gothic romance got harder push in ads like this for *The Mummy*. What matter if cartoon imagery was wildly unrepresentative of what customers saw in the film? It was at least accurate to the spirit of *The Mummy* and decidedly not a sort of love pairing we'd seen on-screen before. There was interest in tombs, mummies, and whatnot thanks to the Tut discovery in 1922 and from that came inevitable notion that a pharaoh or lesser personage could be resurrected. *The Mummy* was properly sold as a love story because it really was that, as opposed to horror along lines of *Dracula* and *Frankenstein*. The chilling cycle and ads for it had come quite a ways in less than two years.

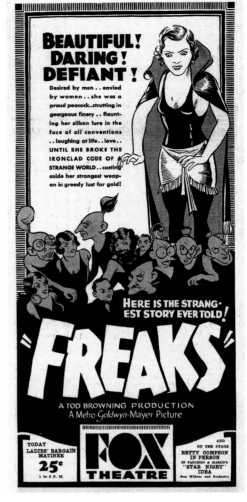

↑

Freaks (1932)

One that went overboard to shock was *Freaks*, excess based on use of real-life monstrosities many in the audience had not seen likes of or even knew existed. The creatures are glimpsed here as cartoons, but no such distance was available in the film. These were actual men without limbs, women conjoined, and gender-confused menagerie with pin heads. You could sell *Freaks* as "The Strangest Story Ever Told" and be entirely right. Then-carnivals still kept such things under canvas, so there were some who'd seen freak shows, but other than past Lon Chaney impersonations, mistakes of nature had not been paraded on-screen before. Ad art, as here, was wiser to play up melodrama and "silken lure" of a recognizably human Leila Hyams rather than unfortunates further down a cast list.

↑
Murders in the Rue Morgue (1932)

"Dracula himself" Bela Lugosi was in again, this time mating virgins with gorillas, or so this ad implies by way of "Whose Bride—Man Or Beast's." Any exploitation campaign had to raise stakes from the last, a principle known since movies began. Copy here is plentiful and crowded, as though the title and Lugosi alone weren't equal to selling task. Was threat of bestiality a strongest lure? "No Children's Prices" suggests they'll not get in for lowered admission or be permitted at all due to *Rue Morgue* content, a teasing play on policy to rouse curiosity. Note the bill's buttress of news, a cartoon, and sport reel plus four acts of vaudeville, not so daunting a program, as *Murders in the Rue Morgue* ran barely over an hour.

↑
The Black Cat (1934)

A web effect often used in chiller layout enhances this ad for the had-to-happen teaming of Boris Karloff with Bela Lugosi. Horror interest was past its peak by 1934, but appetite was still there, as evidenced by future sequels to *Dracula, Frankenstein,* and other of fiends popularized by the early '30s wave. *The Black Cat* had Edgar Allan Poe to further decorate copy, a literary antecedent always useful to legitimize films that bore no relation to his stories otherwise. Karloff and Lugosi had value for their link to the most noteworthy, if not notorious, of first-flush talkie horrors, *Frankenstein* and *Dracula* being names that would be invoked, not just for selling of Karloff/Lugosi down the line, but most of monsters for a next generation.

Promoting One Thing to Sell Another

Commercial tie-in was a gravy bowl for showmen and retailers merging to sell, a device known within the trade as "merchant contact advertising." There was savings for both thanks to sharing of costs plus outreach to a wider public. We saw the preponderance of tie-ins from silent-era ads. The '30s made firmer a handshake between movie and consumer goods, selling of which was enterprise two or more could share.

Harold Lloyd as sales partner to a water heater in ads for 1924's *Hot Water* (see page 33) was but preamble to complex campaigns in which stars and characters they played became guides for major purchasing by viewership, a theatre visit followed hopefully by stop-in with participating dealers and merchants. Did such strategy work? The Mackemer Motor Co. with several then-locations might tell us, but they're as gone to history as Peoria's partnering Princess Theatre and the Ford V-8.

→

Tom Sawyer (1930)

Here is a 1930 instance of Fresno's Fox Wilson Theatre joining hands with Radin & Kamp, "Fresno's Great Christmas Store," on behalf of the retailer's Tom Sawyer outfitting for "real boys." Paramount's sales division and the Elder Manufacturing Company of St. Louis masterminded the nationwide push, Elder having sold its Tom Sawyer garment line since the teens. In this case, Fox Wilson allows Radin & Kamp to dominate its ad, reason perhaps for the department store to pay in full for the newspaper space. Lobby display at the theatre would feature the clothing, while posters for *Tom Sawyer* the movie would festoon the Radin & Kamp boy's department.

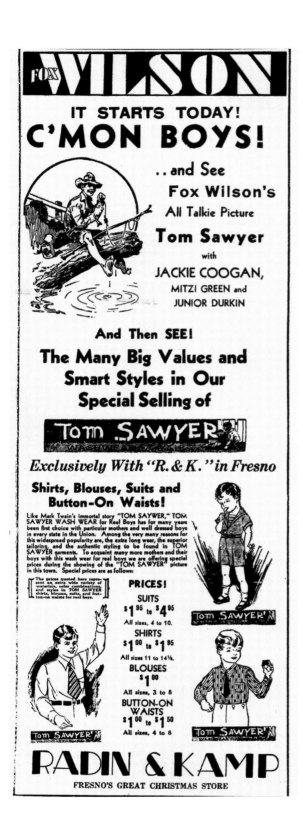

↑
How I Play Golf (1930–31)

How I Play Golf was first in a series of Warner Bros. shorts featuring the famed golfer, Bobby Jones. The sport had become something of a national craze in the early '30s. In fact, miniature golf took meaningful bite out of theatre receipts as many fun seekers took up that pastime rather than moviegoing. Jones cut a striking figure in light sweater and knee breeches, amateur golfers bent upon being as fashionable. To the aid of that objective came Roos Brothers department store of Oakland, California, tying in with the Fox Oakland Theatre to cross-promote sportswear and *How I Play Golf*. There were 10 of these shared ads at total cost of $1,000, which was borne by Roos Brothers, latter getting bulk of emphasis with its $5 sweater as focal point and barest mention of Fox Oakland's bill, which included a Charlie Chan, *The Black Camel*, in addition to *How I Play Golf*.

Looks like a shoe box on wheels to me, but owning a Ford V-8 during the depth of the Depression must have seemed a dream near equal of stardom Robert Young and Barbara Stanwyck enjoyed, and after all, if comic Cliff "Ukulele Ike" Edwards could drive one, why not us? Fulfillment of the dream was as simple as stopping by Mackemer Motor Co. for a test spin, but only after catching *Red Salute* at Peoria's Princess Theatre.

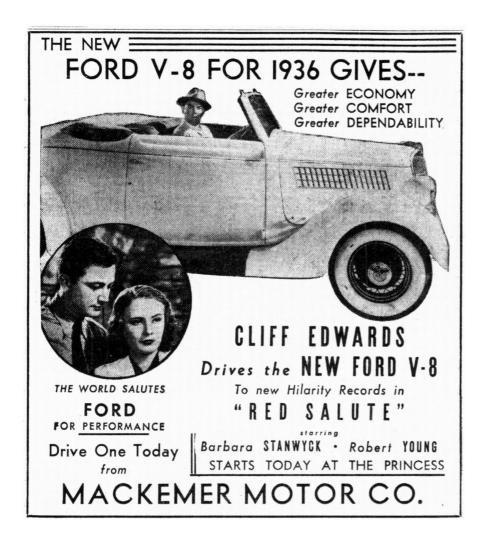

↑
College Swing (1938)

Inviting fans to put themselves in her shoes was effective means by which Betty Grable helped sell footwear, even in prior-to-major-stardom year 1938. Screen personalities wielded their greatest influence with clothing and accessories, these revolving around beauty, primary stock and trade of classic-era movie stars. Hunt's ad features Grable with "rhythm step shoes," Joie Theatre tickets for *College Swing* being given away with each purchase. This ad would have appeared in addition to, if not alongside, Joie's own promotion in Fort Smith, Arkansas, newspapers.

←
The Hurricane (1937)

Lachman Bros. was a leading San Francisco dealer in furniture, carpet, stoves—whatever dressed up a household. They saw value in partnership with showmen and access to patrons who might cook a meal between trips to the Geary Theatre. This ad belongs more to Lachman's than *The Hurricane*, but both would benefit. Detail as to oven features along with "extra liberal terms" seems an odd pairing with Jon Hall and Dorothy Lamour in sarongs, but this ad represents cooperative selling at a peak of efficiency. It would, by the way, occupy a full page in San Francisco newspapers.

Gone to Uncharted Places

Africa was another world then, understood as a place few white men had ever seen. Travel and exploration reels had come out of there, but little by way of sustained narrative. It was for Hollywood to gather resource and nerve to capture raw savagery of this Darkest Continent. Rather than document the landscape, they'd exploit it, Africa a richest backdrop for thrills-a-minute amidst sudden death. The early '30s saw the cycle at fullest bloom, jungle treks running alongside horror films and musical extravagance as chief opiate during hard times.

→

Head Hunters of the South Seas (1922)

Martin Johnson was an explorer whose safaris began where maps ended. He and wife Osa made togetherness pay in terms of his-and-her forays into the unknown. *Head Hunters of the South Seas* wasn't Africa, but peril was as real, headhunters presumed as deadly wherever they did business. This ad has inky depth to set off a bone-in-nose principal as guide to "Tropic Horrors! Devil Dances! Savage Barbarity!" We may assume this was catnip to kids and kids at heart, and we have to wonder who'd even stay to watch "tender love-drama" that was *The Man She Brought Back*—unless he was a cannibal too.

↑

Trader Horn (1931)

The mightiest of jungle thrillers, *Trader Horn* ventured into Africa at dawn of movie sound and came back with miles of bracing footage, which they'd use for not only this film, but *Tarzan, The Ape Man* and sequels to come. *Trader Horn* was promotion's dream, a once-in-lifetime chance to boast every superlative in the kit and be at least half accurate as to each. Audiences really were amazed by this show, and said so in terms of landmark box office for theatres running it.

Best of selling angles was the "White Goddess" pitch, she being alternately "a princess of paganism" or "the cruelest woman in all Africa!"—ad makers taking pick from generous selection. These ads represent the Los Angeles–Hollywood premiere. A first (above left) was prepared by Fox West Coast Theatres for the Grauman's Chinese open, being nude depiction of blonde savage Edwina Booth. The next (above right) is what actually got in print, Ms. Booth with hair splayed decorously to conceal breasts, but compensating in terms of wanton cruelty *Trader Horn* promised. Newspaper advertising had boundaries, and exhibitors would need alternate—as in more discreet—layouts to accommodate local policy.

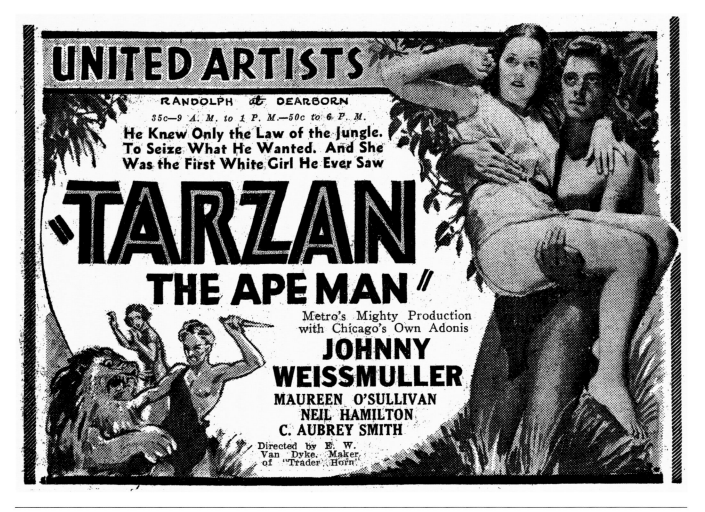

Tarzan, the Ape Man (1932)

Chicago's United Artists Theatre welcomes the "Trader Horn of 1932" with a succession of ads to catalog every thrill found in *Tarzan, The Ape Man*, but note layout's invite for women to compare "mating instinct" of the jungle with tepid options of a civilized society. Here was stealth agenda of showmen who rightly saw sex as surest means to draw distaff half of patronage who had most to do with choosing movies, both for families and couples. United Artists copy was freighted with what amounted to social politics in guise of ballyhoo: "Maybe love was happier when men took their mates like this" and "If all marriages were based on the jungle mating instinct—it would be a happier world." How could husbands or dates stand up to this sort of comparison? Tarzan would be watered down as the Production Code took tighter rein and the series became family friendly, but this first one (and its immediate sequel) revolved first and foremost around Topic A.

Bring 'Em Back Alive (1932)

The essence of all jungle adventure was to show things that "no civilized man had ever seen before." Chief among those who brought footage back lively was Frank Buck, whose biggest of hits, *Bring 'Em Back Alive*, became virtual pseudonym for Buck himself. The picture would stay in circulation for decades thanks to content that didn't date until big studios began taking color cameras to far-off settings. La Salle, Indiana's Majestic Theatre awakens primitive instinct with an ad targeting beasts on rampage and a nubile native unclad. Such was selling of jungle-set adventure in Africa or Malay or wherever features had been made on authentic location.

↑

Trader Horn (Reissue 1953)

Trader Horn came back to a largely indifferent reception in 1953. The picture by then was simply too old, said exhibitors, many of whom would regret booking it. Ads for the reissue reflected far more restrictive ad policy thanks to a Production Code that oversaw not only films, but also their promotion. Edwina Booth in revised art has fur (or is it feathers?) to assure modesty, any suggestion of nudity being out of the question two decades after *Trader Horn*'s initial release.

←

Island of Lost Souls (1933)

By 1933, there was mix and match of genres, the hybrids sometimes effective, other times not. *Island of Lost Souls* was horror's trip to forbidding South Seas and more explicit—some said tastelessly so—than chillers had so far been. The Panther Woman, object of a nationwide talent search, was primarily a selling point. Virtually all ads centered round the "beast-woman" that was progeny of both human and animal. Very atmospheric art for the Paramount Theatre's promotion was supplied by pen/ink whiz Milt Kahl (his sig appears at lower right).

Between the Eyes

The right kind of attraction could be an ad's equivalent of headline news, as evidenced in these shout-outs to Amusement Page viewership. To grab attention and hold it was any layout's objective, as the longer readers looked, the greater their chance of attending. Copy might amount to a challenge or even warning: Miss this show to eventual regret. Ads that hit hardest took a risk of being mocked, but ones that worked made gambles worthwhile.

→

The Trial of Vivienne Ware (1932)

The audience as jury sitters had been tried on radio, and successfully, so the device was brought to film. Decision as to final verdict of *The Trial of Vivienne Ware* is implied as ours, but movies weren't like radio, being a finished product before theatres took charge of them. Vivienne Ware's fate was settled before we bought a ticket, unlike airplays done live where listener or studio audience response could guide the dénouement. Still, the arrow pointing to patron position in the jury box was deft promise that they'd cast a vote as to outcome, even as it was a pledge not kept.

This Seat On The Jury Is Reserved For You!

Come and judge the woman who is accused of murder for love!

Get the inside story of the mystery that thrilled millions of radio listeners!

A million radio listeners were thrilled as this drama of a woman on trial for her life was unfolded before them! As the evidence was presented—they judged the fate of this woman! Now it comes to the screen—more thrillingly told—more dramatic—a human document of life!

"THE TRIAL OF VIVIENNE WARE"
A FOX RADIO DRAMA WITH
JOAN BENNETT
Skeets Gallagher — Zasu Pitts
SUN. MON. TUES.
THE SIGN OF A GOOD TIME!

Paramount
Home of Paramount Pictures

Prices: Mat. 10-15c Till 2 p. m., Then 25c; After 6 p. m., 40c

Added Features!
Boy Friend Comedy "The Knockout"
Screen Souvenirs
Paramount Sound News

↑
Eskimo (1933)

Eskimos as "wife-traders" was essential message of this ad right with the title—should Loew's State have placed it at the top rather than bottom of their display? Maybe "Untamed . . . Unashamed, Unconquerable" was as good, especially with *Eskimo* copy re "their own strange moral code" and payoff below that as to wife swaps. Polar bear attack and a supine female presumably nude beneath shorn fur of the beast make for irresistible art. Loew's makes clever salvage of the semi-documentary that was *Eskimo*.

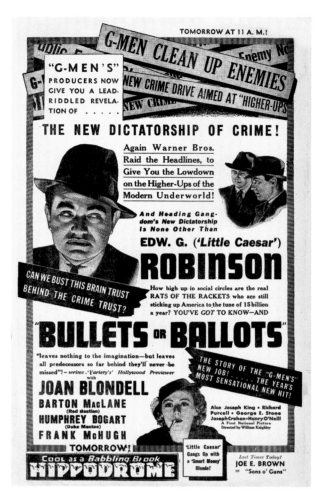

↑
Bullets or Ballots (1936)

Use of headlines off a news page was best means of heralding topical content, just in case the title *Bullets or Ballots* failed to get it done. Real-life desperadoes were shot down daily in 1936 thanks to G-man vigilance, so here was the "cool as a babbling brook" Hippodrome's offer of a badge to crowds fed up with underworld mayhem. Player association with the gangster genre is emphasized from Edward G. Robinson on down—if anyone could pop a cap on bad men, it would be this crew typecast from opposing sides of law.

↑
Exclusive (1937)

Exclusive as a title and "Nerve! She Had It!" as header to femme lead Frances Farmer signals hard-hitting exam of the news game. Insert art makes clear that it's crusading press who'll perform heroism on this Loew's State occasion. Movies, and ads for movies, made it a point to flatter newshounds and publishing apparatus backing them. Most screen treatment of journos was valentines to the trade in observance of codependency between press and film industries.

War Clouds Forming

Bombing of U.S.S. Panay (1937) was up-to-minute screen account of a 1937 incident that drew the United States closer to eventual war with Japan. The Panay, a U.S. Navy gunboat anchored in China, was air attacked and sunk by Japanese forces, the latter claiming not to have seen American flags painted on the deck. "The Attack That Shook a World" then became basis for Universal's 30-minute documentary (Not a Newsreel!), which led the bill in ads like this one. Sensational news events could be viewed only on theatre screens during those years before television.

Selling Something Special

To make your message effective was sometimes to vary it. The right attraction could be sold outside the box, as could novelties on tap: critic hurrahs, Technicolor, even a director deemed strong enough to hypo box office. This, then, was imagination's preserve, a spot for showmen to use the noodle to step off worn paths and take layout where it hadn't laid before.

→

Design for Living (1933)

A marching-toward-camera cast was not unusual to publicize new releases, though the device was less often used in ads. Here, then, was exception on two counts, second being *Design for Living*'s director among glamour lineup. Ernst Lubitsch had been a meaningful name since coming to America 10 years before. Known for on-set flamboyance, the ever-present cigar, and style that became known as "The Lubitsch Touch," this was one back-of-camera face Amusement Page readers, at least those in Manhattan, would recognize. *Design for Living* was here making its Gotham bow, on roadshow basis, at Broadway's Criterion Theatre, where it could truthfully boast of being "the only theatre in the world showing this picture this year" as it opened 12/29/33.

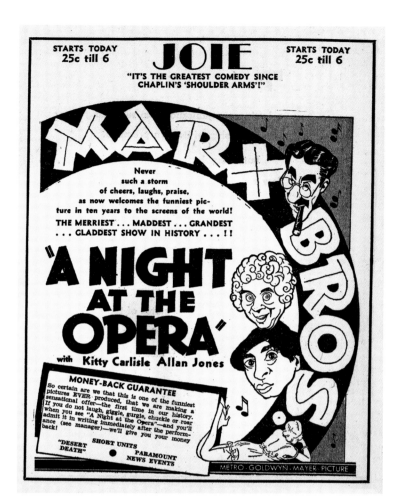

←
A Night at the Opera (1935)

The "money back guarantee" could be a tricky device, yet theatres continued using it where a good time was most assured. Anyone seeking a refund had to run gauntlet of close interrogation, plus swear in writing that *A Night at the Opera* had not once made them giggle, gurgle, chortle, etc. Was such ordeal justified to get that quarter admission back? Few, if any, in Fort Smith, Arkansas, would want to admit having no sense of humor whatever, let alone sign an affidavit to that effect, so the Joie's gamble was likely a safe one.

↓
Follow the Fleet (1936)

Chicago's RKO Palace had a novel approach here: Make the Astaire-Rogers musical a headline event, at least in terms of a third-week holdover ad where urgency is lent to fact this will be the final stanza for *Follow the Fleet*. The style was a grabber among conventional promos as put forth by competing theatres. By a following week, several might use the same headline device, or maybe the RKO Palace cribbed it off someone else's ad from the past week. Such was the promotional well from which all layout artists drank.

The humble Jeffris Theatre in Janesville, Wisconsin, faced the same Depression woe as virtually all venues—attendance down and overhead exceeding admissions. How to hypo the house? One notion was to give away money—bribe them, in effect, to come see a show and hope for a "bank night" win. Prize of $150 would buy groceries for a season in 1936 or put substantial down payment on a Studebaker. Either way, it was heady inducement to go see Boris Karloff in whatever mischief he was up to, thoughts/dreams centered on instant wealth as *The Walking Dead* unspooled. The Jeffris ad wisely puts the cash lure at front and center here, copy reading more like a racing form than promotion for films.

↑
Lost Horizon (1937)

It was possible by 1937 to sell a film on Frank Capra's name. He had directed the astounding hit that was *It Happened One Night* and had a shelf full of awards. Capra's was a common touch that reached every kind of audience, so it was safe selling him as prime reason to come see a show. *Lost Horizon* would break his string of successes, but going in it looked like the greatest of all the director had done. The Geary was Frisco-based and threw this "tribute to a genius" with assist of stars who had worked with Capra or hoped they eventually would. Note roadshow policy and advanced admission; this was a signal event for San Francisco and the Geary.

↑
God's Country and the Woman (1937)

How valued was the novelty of Technicolor by exhibitors? This ad from Keith's 105th in Cleveland gives us a tip. The improved process, as recently utilized by features, lent three colors rather than accustomed two to viewing palette, along with subtle gradations between. Technicolor could be a stunning process where properly used and presented. Keith's promotes the rainbow here as "all-new" and "true," which in 1937 it was. *God's Country and the Woman* was among first to present Technicolor on full-length terms.

Maid of Salem (1937)

Another director was spotlighted in an ad, only this one hasn't held his fame like Lubitsch. Frank Lloyd had a '30s box office record of Best Picture winners like *Cavalcade* and *Mutiny on the Bounty*, so audiences saw his name touted in press and fan mags covering Hollywood. Loew's State pictures Lloyd as architect behind *Maid of Salem*, examining footage as leads Claudette Colbert and Fred MacMurray look on. Lloyd is also most prominently featured in the ad's copy, making this an atypical-for-the-'30s celebration of a director at expense of stars.

Call of the Yukon (1938)

From high to low on ticket pricing, here was desperate measure taken by the Embassy Theatre in Brooklyn, a staving off of loss, or perhaps closure, by means of lowered admissions. That of course is emphasis of this ad that otherwise promotes a pair of "B" actioners, neither of which could singly sustain the bill. Pricing in 1938 was such as to make 20 cents for a matinee seem fair; a dime for kids at all times was hardly more than venues two decades before had got. The Embassy's choice was the same as any struggling house: Adapt or perish.

The double-feature "menace" (as tagged by the film companies) was deplored by everyone but the customers. By the late '30s, most theatres were obliged to offer two-for-one and perceived "more for your money." *Juarez* was a big picture, however, long in run time and elevated as to content. Could the Gillioz Theatre in Springfield, Missouri, offer their program both ways and spare dignified watchers the indignity of seeing *Juarez* with lowly "B" that was *Sudden Money*? This was called "a new trial policy," but we have to wonder how many patrons willingly forfeited an extra movie for the same priced ticket.

Here in the Flesh

Screen personalities were other-worldly enough to inspire awe when one of them made landfall at local theatres. A big-enough name easily trumped whatever was on screens for a week of personal appearing. Ads had but to place the famed face front and prominent, then let local fan base do the rest. Local press was dependable for "news" of a celebrity arrival, this more valued exposure than any paid publicity. There had been star apps going back to the teens, but the '30s saw touring reach a crest. Many luminaries had their start at vaudeville in any case, so could manage 20 or so minutes of satisfactory amusement. Ones who sang or danced fared best. All knew the meaning of 14-hour days under hot lights and were equal to the exhaustion of repeated live shows.

→

Mae Murray (1929)

Mae Murray was pretty much done with movies by the early '30s, or, rather, they were done with her. She'd been temperamental and burned studio bridges, but plain folks in sufficient number remembered Hollywood's "Merry Widow" (her most famous role) and were intrigued besides by her princess title bestowed by marriage to royalty of dubious origin. Mae kept faith with fans by putting on a good show and making nice with ones who sought a handshake. Albee's Cincinnati venue was for vaudeville since 1892, but in 1929 became part of RKO's chain and home to fresh talkies like *Lucky Boy* and remnants of a stage glory the Albee name once represented. Princess Murray's "exquisite dance" is balanced by "feminine gymnasts" and "vaudeville's little buffoon" Sylvia Clark, the bill and ad as always dedicated to something for everyone.

The Marx Brothers (1930)

The Four Marx Brothers found touring remunerative between pictures for Paramount, their appearance like a sprinkle of big-time Broadway upon local stages. These boys were a sure thing among other live acts plus a feature film and would not be taxed beyond 20 or so minutes performing, even with spots repeated through the day per Cleveland's RKO Palace schedule. The ad makes the most of its Marxes by framing each with a star, the team sold as individual attractions and thus four times the value of solo celebrities offered by rival houses. The Palace is positioned too as site for further names (Ted Lewis, Ruth Etting, others) and one of but four stops the Marx Bros. will make on their 1930 live circuit.

←

Olsen and Johnson (1932)

All-comedy, that is, laughs on both stage and screen, were sure getters during an era when theatres were as much party as place to passively view. In this instance, festivity began in the RKO Mainstreet's outer lobby, where live broadcast sent performers and arriving patronage over airwaves to bid listeners leave chairs at home and come occupy ones at the theatre. Radio was often a pied piper to movies, especially where getting to the show was mere matter of catching a streetcar or even walking to where fun was had. Olsen and Johnson were "nut" comedians whose wildness spilled off prosceniums and into the audience, their "Atrocities of 1932" a sure antidote to hard times. The Mainstreet puts smiling faces, both photographic and cartoon, at service of "the greatest show we've had," which maybe it was, judging by mirth promised here.

→

Ben Bernie (1933)

"The Old Maestro" Ben Bernie was one of radio's early musical host successes, his a following that could reliably fill seats wherever his troupe appeared. Bernie kept music at center, salted his orchestra with eccentrics for humor's sake ("all the lads"), with performance not unlike Kay Kyser the following decade. His airwave sponsor, Pabst Blue Ribbon, gets ad mention, which may have been contractual, as Bernie and their beer were interlocked since lift of Prohibition enhanced public profile of both. A screen show, with feature, shorts, and news, seems almost incidental to the Bernie splash.

←

Amos 'n' Andy (1934)

Another booked into the RKO Palace was radio's biggest noise, Amos 'n' Andy, members of the family to most households and a guaranteed house-filler wherever they'd appear live. The ad makes clear that the two will represent an entire cast of characters from the show (Kingfish, Lightnin', Madame Queen), Freeman Gosden and Charles Correll lending voice for the lot, in addition to corking themselves up as onstage Amos n' Andy. Here was where radio sleight of hand had to be explained in order for the act to make sense, but audiences didn't mind the peek behind on-air curtain it afforded. Freeman and Gosden essentially were doing the job of a whole troupe of performers, and their impersonations were much enjoyed by crowds unaware that these two were behind the voices of so many. Amos 'n' Andy are thus not only themselves, but the whole of the wildly popular show's cast.

↓

Buddy Rogers (1934)

Charles "Buddy" Rogers was a performer who could do anything, play any instrument, and top anyone else's show. He'd been a juvenile star at Paramount, "America's Boyfriend" from onset of talkies, an apostle of pep and antidote to the Crash. His film success had passed its peak by 1934, but there was radio and live opportunity such as here at the RKO Palace, where Rogers would have morning start, then pull plow through 12 exhausting hours to follow, his only relief the supporting "cavaliers of radio fame" and unspool of *Coming Out Party*. Rogers' head shot is nicely juxtaposed with band art, the dancing figure looking up at him, and cartoon capture from the film. The Palace's artist came nicely prepared to this duty.

←

Thurston (1935)

A magician who was good enough could top the bill in any house, stage illusions being sure attraction going back centuries. Houdini had been a most famed practitioner, Thurston among successors and by 1935 a "baffler" supreme offering on-stage vivisection, a stunt to surpass even his sawing of a woman in half. Was vivisection a familiar term to audiences? They'd know at least that it represented something disagreeable to human bodies, which were objects of Thurston's exercise. These magic shows were as much to shock as instill a sense of wonder, being scarier at times than horror films on screen. Many a "spook show" was hosted by illusionists. Buffalo's Shea Theatre posits pointy-ear devils to convey uncanny aspect of Thurston marvels. Maybe Rudy Vallee and his *Sweet Music* were needed to calm nerves after such an exhibition.

←

Betty Boop (1935)

Sometimes even a cartoon character could assume flesh-and-blood proportion on theatre stages. Betty Boop was animator Max Fleischer's creation and property of Paramount. Her voice was rendered by Mae Questel (sic in the ad, her name more exotically spelled "Questelle"). The act would amount to Mae coming out in Boop attire, doing time-honored Boopisms, a few songs, then cede to others of vaudeville lineup (would she upstage Loyalta's Arabian Stallions or vice versa?). Shea's Buffalo Theatre uses the drawn Betty Boop as opposed to art of Questel, the cartoon recognizable, whereas she was not. Balance of art is well maintained, the two Boops looking at each other across the ad so as to keep focus on copy.

↑

Stepin Fetchit (1935)

A different Palace, but entertainment still palatial, as beloved character comedian Stepin Fetchit does his "Slow Motion" act to live-wire accompany of band, dancing, and "a bevy of gorgeous creole beauties." Step needed fast steppers to offset snail pace of his own routine, which worked best in tandem with quicker-footed support. It was enough just to see him live, however, for Fetchit by the mid-'30s was among top draws below the title of films where he appeared, most notably the Will Rogers series for Fox. In this onstage instance, Fetchit is star attraction, *The Case of the Lucky Legs* a programmer best offered as second feature or support to a stage program as here.

↑

Vaudeville with College Scandal (1935)

Straight vaudeville as partner to screen entertainment was policy at many houses right through the '30s and '40s, and even into the '50s in some instances. Acts were booked plentiful and, for the most part, cheap, object being to give more (or at least impression of more) for admission coin. Whether the four Albee Sisters were "world famous" might be revealed through further research, but chances are their fame was confined to landscape of tank towns and theatres like the Cecil, seating 859 and located in Mason City, Iowa. So, how would a puppet show play to even an auditorium modest as the Cecil's, unless they were *very* large puppets? The ad makes the most of the five acts, and there is *College Scandal* for support, not so big a feature as Friday's departing *Anna Karenina*, which probably didn't need vaudeville to fill seats.

↑
Major Bowes Amateurs (1935)

Sometimes the big name was an emcee rather than performer. Major Bowes was known as a discoverer of talent, his radio program a clearinghouse for non-pros seeking to break into biz by copping a weekly amateur prize. The best of Bowes' talent took to roads with him, these not leading to stardom perhaps, but to gratification at least that came of applause from audiences. Local hosts would offer up their own amateurs to buttress Bowes' ensemble, as here at Toledo's Paramount Theatre. Twenty-two acts "in person" kept each performance brief at least, in case any proved punk, and naturally there was screen support for added insurance.

Beauty Served by the Ton

Of freak attractions, here was a freakiest. Promoter Billy Watson made a career of touring with bountiful beauties such as shown here, this 1936 "Beef Trust" weighing heavy on bills his ensemble couldn't help but dominate.

↑

Jackie Coogan and Betty Grable (1937)

What Jackie Coogan didn't know about performing, nobody did. He'd been at it since babyhood, cutting teeth with Charlie Chaplin as title character in *The Kid*, which most still remembered late as 1937 when he and wife Betty Grable took comedy-and-dance on tour, Jackie an oldest of hands at vaudeville. This ad could trade on both *The Kid* and the couple's visibility in collegiate musicals at Paramount. They were popular, if not "Hollywood's most famous sweethearts," and had youthful pep, both serving needs of a quick-paced stage shenanigan. Coogan/Grable being vets of film made behind-scenes Hollywood a natural format, this plus the collegiate angle well emphasized in the Palace's ad.

↑

Cab Calloway (1937)

A real force of nature in jumpin' jive, "his hi-de-highness of ho-de-ho" was guarantor of a full house most everywhere he went through the '30s. The Cab Calloway format was night club bred, but translated easily to presentation houses where he'd be flash point of each show, with movies a mere chaser. The Palace need hardly mention *Melody for Two*, a tepid sidebar to Calloway and his Cotton Club Revue. Advertising wisely puts him full-length with baton; it understood that Cab as conductor was fullest entertainment in itself. Note use of dark background and well-placed ovals, with the cartooned dancer, to put across all elements of the bill.

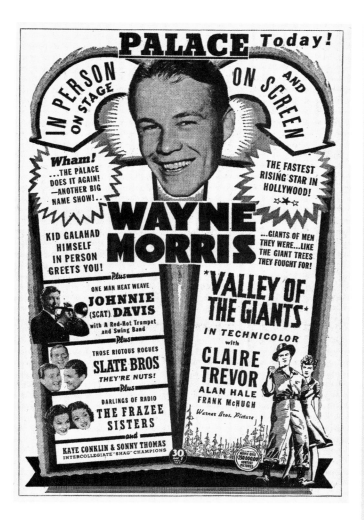

↑
Wayne Morris (1938)

Here's where theatres held hands tightest with Hollywood industry. Wayne Morris was a Warner Bros. discovery pushed up the studio ladder toward major stardom (which he never truly achieved), but getting him closer to a responding public needed not only film parts, but live appearing so that "Kid Galahad" Morris could "greet" customers to the Palace. The "wham" was in having him on screen in a new Technicolor production, plus the actor pressing flesh and signing stills in outer lobbies. Stars, if not born, often could be made by such process. The Palace hedged bets by backing Morris with four vaude acts, one of which, Johnnie "Scat" Davis, was known and liked from Hollywood musicals. Dynamic arrows pointing out and downward from Morris are effective statement that his would be a name and face for moviegoers to reckon with.

There's Gonna Be a Fight

Another look way back was this recap of July 4, 1919's heavyweight match between Jack Dempsey and Jess Willard, a brawl old-timers would recall and 1939 youth might find amusing. Antique reels were fun as novelties, so long as they didn't outstay welcome. This one would have been on and off within eight minutes, just enough to give the flavor of the fight before 1939's *We Are Not Alone*.

→ The Buccaneer (1938)

Atlanta's Fox Theatre got signal privilege of world premiering the mighty DeMille special that was *The Buccaneer* in 1938. A premiere was only as good as its celebrity guests, however, and here was one that delivered fully to Atlanta expectation. They'd not see an opening this big until the following year's *Gone With the Wind*. DeMille himself was a grandest catch of the Big Night, his star brighter than most Hollywood players thanks to his weekly hosting of the Lux Radio Theatre, with its airwave dramatization of outstanding films. DeMille players on hand at the Fox were not leads from *The Buccaneer*, but known character faces and a starlet (Evelyn Keyes) under personal contract to C.B. The combination of these plus a big picture debut made for memorable show-going in Atlanta.

→ Bob Hope (1940)

The concept of transplanting radio to theatre stages was popular from the start of home listening. Airwave personalities would simply duplicate their program before a live audience; sometimes, in fact, they'd broadcast from the stage. Bob Hope by 1940 was comedy's leading light in movies and radio, each promoting the other to benefit of both. Cleveland's Palace Theatre was welcoming Bob back to home ground, since he'd grown up at the Palace and local venues where ambition took early hold. Five stage shows a day was exhausting for even a trouper with Hope's energy, let alone his "riotous radio gang" expected to sing/dance/amuse on repeat basis. Those morning stands were especially tough, what with smaller and less responsive crowds spread across Palace cavern of 3,284 seats.

Leave the Children Home

Pitching sleaze pics to mainstream news readers was as much a matter of caution as showmanship. Children were most avid for what was playing, and little saucer eyes blinded by blue ads could mean the slap of an ad ban on offending theatre men. It's remarkable that artists got away with as much as they did, though maybe ease came of bad apples being few in otherwise clean barrels. Outlaw venues had to make a living too, after all. Their advertising was closest to the lowly pitch heard on carnival midways, which everyone knew and, for the most part, tolerated. Most arresting of layouts were often those that disguised trash as uplift, as in "see this and be better for it," or "bring your daughters—they should know." Sex and Shame led the mix, with half-man/half-gorilla, drug scaring, or vice exposé for sidebars. Whatever was most forbidden sold best to its target audience, but that bull's-eye stayed small as families shied away.

↑

Ingagi (1930)

This was jungle rot with most of its footage faked, but there was one trick in the bag that all advertising bowed to: native women sacrificed to and carried off by a "giant gorilla" that answered to Ingagi, the name of which would become a '30s catchphrase among titillated youth who'd somehow snuck in to see the lurid farrago. Human-beast coupling, implied but certainly not shown, would fan darkest corners of audience imagination, making *Ingagi* a freak hit to net reputed millions. The idea was a sound one and would be back as basis for 1933's mainstream *King Kong*. The Palace acknowledges "claims" of *Ingagi* scenes that were "an almost impossibility," which indeed they were proven to be, but who cared by such time as cash registers were filled, then emptied, by off-to-the-bank exhibs?

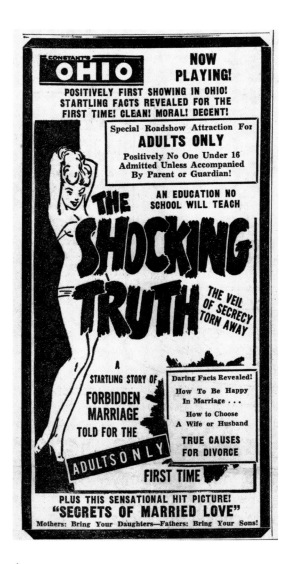

↑

The Shocking Truth (1933)

Clean! Moral! and Decent! seem inconsistent with an attraction called *The Shocking Truth*, which in less shocking truth was 1933 oldie *Damaged Lives*, a here-retitled exploiter of venereal disease. That one traveled for decades under a dizzying variety of labels; whoever owned *Damaged Lives* seems to have made the most of it, the film maintaining interest today for being directed by cultist fave Edgar G. Ulmer. Constant's Ohio Theatre was located in Steubenville of that state, better recalled as singer Dean Martin's hometown. Could he have been among youth brought by their fathers to see *The Shocking Truth* and its "sensational" co-hit, *Secrets of Married Love*?

↑

Illegal Doctor (1930s)

This seems to be some sort of alternate title, and sure enough no trace of *Illegal Doctor* exists in reference guides. Should sleeves have been rolled higher and searches deeper? Maybe this is one where the juice just isn't worth the squeeze, as how many actually care over *Illegal Doctor*'s origin or correct moniker? Noteworthy is fact they ran the thing at Kearny Burlesk, inquiry revealing its location in San Francisco. Live burlesque plus *Illegal Doctor* must have been fillip to the senses even for keyhole peepers at the Kearny.

←↑
Ecstasy (1933)

Ecstasy was a notorious import long before Hedy Lamarr arrived on U.S. shores. It was refused a mainstream release by the Production Code Administration, and theatres wedded to that authority would not play the Czechoslovakian film. Some independents bucked the trend in hope of realizing profit that would come of a "hot film" that had been suppressed, even burned, in one well-publicized incident. The Royal Theatre in Kansas City took a chance, kept youngsters out ("No Children's Admissions"), and traded boldly on outrage swirling around *Ecstasy*. The Royal, which sat 1,132, was very much home to family audiences, so here was a maverick move bound to stir local controversy. Success of *Ecstasy* elsewhere, however, made it a gamble worth taking.

↑

Engagi (1934)

"Engagi" was no less a misnomer than "Ingagi" since neither name stood for anything at all, at least in African language from which they allegedly derived, but his/its being here in person, even if a mere man draped in fur, was enough to set rows of youth upon paroxysm of joy. As for Engagi having come "direct from (the) century of progress," we can but speculate as to what progress amounted to in 1934.

↑

Smashing the Vice Trust (1937)

The angle was this: girls kidnapped from high school, or was it high-school girls kidnapped? Anyhow, they're forced into brothels. Frisco's Davies Theatre treads lightly on the sex theme to emphasize "G-Men and police in their battle against . . . the underworld." Had there been a recent rile over too-tawdry ads for this sort of exploitation? There's at least cartoon imagery of scant-clad cuties to keep the faith.

←

Black Legion (1937)

Sometimes a mainstream pic would tickle edges of exploitation, as here with Warner's *Black Legion,* another that tore headlines off a front page and flung same at presumably shocked populace. *Black Legion* would operate strictly within Production Code limits as subscribed to by all major film companies, but its heart—and advertising—was very much with junk dealers who knew what tags like "talk and die" could accomplish. "Hooded hoodlums" as referenced was a real-life terror group that operated in heartland U.S. until state and federal authority stamped PAID to their outlawry.

Offering a new star was normally a slow, if not cautious, process. Audiences didn't like idols pushed on them. Here, however, was an exception. Linda Darnell's celebrity would be fait accompli from her first picture, *Hotel for Women* (1939), thanks to resolve of her creators at 20th Century Fox. Cleveland's Palace Theatre and thousands like it would duly announce Darnell and await applause. "You Know A New Star When You See One" was attempt at flattering patrons, as if they'd have something to do with Darnell celebrity to come. Actually they did, of course. Rejection of *Hotel for Women* and its new discovery would have meant fast fade for both.

They Won't Let It Go

Holdovers were a sure way of conveying hits. A show kept beyond its planned engagement told the town that here was something they *must* see, for look at the crowds that already had. Ads pictured eager attendees, lines in wait for an attraction the hosting theatre could not part with. In fact, most holdovers were planned with multiple days or weeks agreed upon or reduced to booking contract well in advance of opening. What mattered was instilling urgency to see a film ad-alleged to be the talk of the town.

→

Born to Dance (1936)

"Of Course It Stays!" was an expression frequently used, inferring prior knowledge to the reader that, yes, everyone knows *Born to Dance* is a hit, and those who haven't laid down coin are badly out of touch. "See It Again!" is given emphasis by twice-mention in copy, with further inducement of a new co-feature, *Rose Bowl*, brought in for the second week to freshen the bill.

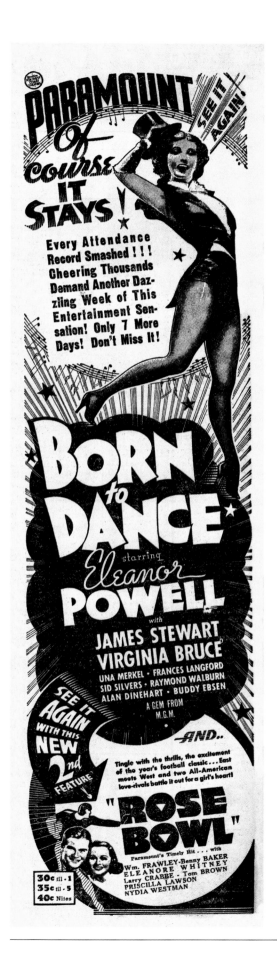

↑
Lost Horizon (1937)

Larger theatres could boast of "thousands" that demand a holdover, this
believable because such palaces did seat thousands. The "X" over Deanna
Durbin's face plays cheeky sport with ad convention—had a vandal taken
pen to San Francisco's Amusement Page? Specialness of four-week play
is emphasized by the pledge that *Lost Horizon* won't be back in Frisco for
two months. Nature of run-zone-clearance policy as observed by large city
theatres made this no idle threat. Miss *Lost Horizon* this time and you'll wait
long to see it.

A biggest event for towns and cities was grand opening of a new theatre. Modernistic design was the byword of '30s building—or refurbish—of showplaces. "Iced Air" was bow to expectation that auditoriums be a zone of comfort year-round, this a priority along with seating to ease stress on backsides (older patrons had not forgotten hard surface, or even benches, from nickelodeons of yore). The "New" Palace Theatre of Fort Worth, Texas, around since the teens, was here celebrating a 1936 face-lift, while New Orleans' brand-new Circle Theatre opened doors in 1939. Note Circle mention of merchants and suppliers that took part in construction, and fact, mentioned three times in the ad, that this would be a racially integrated venue.

NEW ORLEANS' *newest and most modern*

AIR CONDITIONED BY FRIGIDAIRE

CIRCLE THEATRE

ST. BERNARD AVENUE at NORTH GALVEZ STREET

CIRCLE

OPENS TOMORROW!

At 5 P. M.
DOORS OPEN 4:45

With the splendid co-operation of skilled workmanship, quality material and service rendered by the firms listed below, the Circle Theatre opens its doors to the white and colored public of New Orleans with one of the most modern and up-to-the-minute theatres in the city.

Handsomely appointed with a large, roomy, maple-chair seating capacity designed for your comfort . . . Luxurious carpets throughout the theatre, beautiful smoking lounges with deep-cushioned chairs for both white and colored guests. Indirect lighting in the newest Flourescent Lighting equipment. The latest RCA Photophone and Boothe equipment has been installed. Completely Air-Conditioned in the proper temperature by a gigantic Frigidaire Air-Cooling system.

It is truly the show place of this city where you may relax in comfort and be thoroughly entertained!

SHOW STARTS AT 5 P. M. DAILY
SUNDAY 2 P. M.

Frigidaire
4436 Toulouse St.

Olympia Roofing Co.
1025 Toulouse St.

Southern Concrete Products Co.
4516 D'Hemecourt St.

Standard Paint Shop
223 S. Rocheblave St.

Industrial Electric, Inc.
3227 Magazine St.

Herman T. Makofsky
General Contractor
3034 Palmyra St.

National Theatre Supply Co.
220 S. Liberty St.

Elmer Candy Co., Inc.
540 Magazine St.

Lob Insurance Agency
Hibernia Bldg.

National Sash & Door Co.
600 N. Dupre St.

Clerc Foundations, Inc.
Maritime Bldg.

Tile Shop
824 Carondelet St.

Grimaldi Plumbing Co.
719 Royal St.

Jno. Worner & Son, Inc.
Hardware—1019 Bienville St.

American Heating & Plumbing Co., Inc.
829 Baronne St.

Frank P. Fischer Engineering Co.
Janitrol Unit Heaters
920 Tchoupitoulas St.

RCA PHOTOPHONE Equipment

—ADDED SHORTS—
Erskine Hawkins'
"DEVILED HAM"

"FERDINAND THE BULL"
In Technicolor

Gigantic FRIGIDAIRE Air-Conditioning System

What men will do for a woman like this!

'THEY MADE ME A CRIMINAL'

JOHN GARFIELD
Surpassing even the great promise of his performance in "Four Daughters"...with the

"DEAD END" KIDS
CLAUDE RAINS · ANN SHERIDAN
MAY ROBSON ·
GLORIA DICKSON

For White and Colored

Daily 5 P. M.
Sunday 2 P. M.

Newest FLOURESCENT Lighting

→

Angels with Dirty Faces (1938)

If 75,000 say a show is good, who are we to argue? Here's instance of peer (or patron) pressure brought to bear on Clevelanders who'd not yet caught *Angels with Dirty Faces*. What was their excuse for not joining in? Again, the numerical device worked, as the Hippodrome sat 3,592.

→

Babes in Arms (1939)

The Capitol in New York was Loew's flagship, promotion ideas developed there sent far/ wide to other venues owned by the company. This word-of-mouth gag was ideal accompany to announcement of a holdover. Was everyone talking about *Babes in Arms*? According to this cartoon, yes they were!

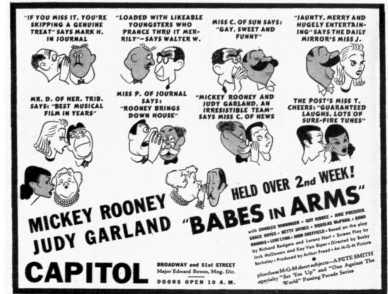

←

Andy Hardy Gets Spring Fever (1939)

Pin a medal on whatever art shop dreamed this up: Mickey Rooney's Andy Hardy blocking entrance to a crowd-choked Loew's that even Robert Taylor, Hedy Lamarr, Lew Ayres, and Lana Turner can't penetrate. A 2nd Big Week of *Andy Hardy Gets Spring Fever* plus "Lots of Hits . . . on the Way" was ad psychology to instill moviegoing habit in much of a 1939 populace, each big show feeding into the next.

←

The Wizard of Oz (1939)

Photo proof of crowds swarming Chicago's United Artists Theatre, along with tornado motif inspired by the film, helped make an urban hit of *The Wizard of Oz* in 1939. It was hinterland drop-off and unusually high negative cost that put MGM's musical in the red.

Stars to Bait the Hook

Movies had a star system in place since the teens. By the '30s, it was recognized as exhibition's best partner for promoting films. Nothing trumped faces as focal point of a layout. Hollywood and a fan press took credit for creation of stars, but more famed names got that way thanks to local ads addressing readers on a daily basis. Magazines and filmland publicity may have made the introductions, but it was individual theatres that would close the sale, their print promotion usually a final contact made before customer met cashier.

→

Pardon Us (1931)

It was something of an event when Stan Laurel and Oliver Hardy made their first feature-length comedy. The pair lent themselves to caricature art, that being shorthand to promote L&H since they'd gotten together in the '20s. *Pardon Us* ran but an hour, so a volley of short subjects, or in Loew's State's instance, vaudeville, was needed to fill out the program.

The Private Life of Henry VIII (1933)

Here was something of a freak success from England, that country's biggest-selling export so far. Charles Laughton was known to U.S. audiences, having made several features stateside by 1933, so his image was useful to ad placement. Note too the use of Mae West and Clark Gable for modern comparison to Henry VIII's lovemaking prowess. Chicago's United Artists Theatre did not want *The Private Life of Henry VIII* confused with typical art films from offshore, even if it did traffic in costumes and accents.

The Thin Man (1934)

First of a series, but that wasn't understood in 1934 when this opener arrived. The Loew's Grand trades on prominence of the source novel by Dashiell Hammett and its potential appeal to women. William Powell and the book cover are centered, while copy promises "dashing, racy" situations. Release of *The Thin Man* would come but a couple months before tightening of the Production Code, and that put "paid" to much that was dashing or racy in movies.

↑

Mutiny on the Bounty (1935)

A pair of ads from Loew's State emphasize the grandeur of MGM's biggest 1935 release. The sailor's knot as border would offset this display from others on an Amusement Page, and none could boast spending of two million or as many years spent in production. Aside from that, of course, it was stars that would sell *Mutiny on the Bounty*, principally Clark Gable, "the girl that got" him being pictured, but not named.

↑

Dionne Quintuplets (1935)

There were also stars of shorter term, novelty if not freak attractions. One was the Dionne Quintuplets (or better put, Five), born 5/28/34, and immediately co-opted by Hollywood for a group of short subjects, then features. Any footage of these miracle babies was gold in the till for showmen. The Quints in a single reel as offered by the Keith's 105th Theatre (Cleveland) was a lure to surpass tepid feature *Hell in the Heavens*.

↑
Swing Time (1936)

Smack in the middle of Astaire-Rogers mania came this possibly best of their dance musicals. Most perceptive of ad makers put the team head-to-foot in midst of doing what both did best. Movement to rhythm was what A&R's public bought tickets for, comedy and romance secondary to signature dancing. Cleveland's Hippodrome ad escorts our view along a ribbon of lead names, down to the film title and a supporting cast against starry background with surround of musical notes. A model ad, generated in-house by Hipp staff.

↑
One in a Million (1936)

Another who danced, with added novelty of doing so on ice and in skates, was Sonja Henie, whose *very* major stardom from the mid-'30s into the '40s has been pretty much forgotten since. Fox made her vehicles, lent the Norwegian-born Gold Medalist low comic support of the Ritz Brothers, and saw *One in a Million* earn rentals upward of $2 million worldwide. The Keith's ad is vividly highlighted by a pen-and-ink Henie posed full-length with skating chorus below, effective shorthand for the new star's appeal in her first American film.

Oh, How Rudy Could Love!

The name of Rudolph Valentino could still quicken pulses more than a decade after his passing. The Studio was a Chicago art house and no stranger to offbeat programming. Their ad centers Valentino, but does not ridicule him—wise policy as fans even by 1938 wouldn't warm to their idol being mocked. Besides, there was humor built into *Son of the Sheik* and *The Eagle*, the pair meant not to be taken too seriously, even when they were new.

↖ ←

Institutional Ads

Star merchandising, like star creation, was for the most part done closer to home. Film companies with players on payroll kept each in the public's sight line via institutional ads, such as these that appeared in fan magazines and wider-circulated monthlies. The idea was less to sell individual names than the factory that presented them, each of studios proposing its contract list as most imposing. Producer/Distributors and exhibitors they dealt with rose or fell with allure the stars brought to marquees, so it was crucial for Paramount, MGM, and the rest to maintain healthy stables of popular faces.

1939's Would-Be Snow White

Ads for the Disney *Snow White and the Seven Dwarfs* revolved in large part around the Dwarfs. Some of them left off Snow White entirely. Paramount would rush out *Gulliver's Travels* in hopes of same reward and to beat Disney's *Pinocchio* into theatres. Note dense surround of Gulliver here by cartoony figures not unlike the Dwarfs. Marketers knew these would be principal lure to *Gulliver's Travels*.

1940s

Business Booms and Ads Peak

When It Looked Like Prosperity
Would Last Forever

Filmgoing had been popular before, but never like this. The '40s and onset of war made movies the drug of choice for many more millions than theatres had accommodated before. Round-clock schedules saw seating filled morning through nights, this a happy by-product of disposable cash from three shifts performing war work. Outcome of America's fight was uncertain and that lent urgency to films depicting the struggle. No more were movies a light amusement, what with newsreels dispensing combat footage and even musicals and comedies doubling down on audience emotions.

Ads reached a crest here. Print progress made them look the best ever on Amusement Pages. Layout artists who'd been at it 20 or more years lent fruits of that experience to daily galleries of advertising at its most accomplished and sophisticated. World War II was like electric current plugged into promotion, all stops out where it came to rousing patriotism and vilifying our enemies. Such ads would be plenty incendiary if used today. Not so, then. Victory was the goal, and film ads paved a straightest road toward it.

→

Devil Dogs of the Air (1934/1942)

An antique hauled from storage now that we were fighting again, 1934's *Devil Dogs of the Air* was actually a peacetime service story where not a hostile shot was fired, though you'd not figure so from this ad's depiction of '40s-modern aircraft zooming toward objective. The word "again" is cited thrice, but were customers sufficiently clued as to *Devil*'s being eight years old?

→

I Cover the War! (1937) and Saboteur (1942)

War clouds rained war-themed pics in that first year of conflict. Demand for a while outstripped supply, so oldies came (back) to fill the breach, in this case a 1937 John Wayne actioner, *I Cover the War!*, which actually dealt with Arab uprisings against occupying British. It at least had action plus reasonable bloodletting to serve in tandem with fresher product that was Alfred Hitchcock's *Saboteur*.

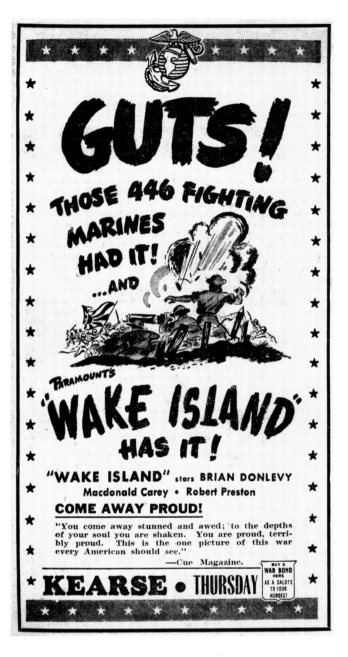

↑

Wake Island (1942)

We took a pasting at Wake, plus lots of other zones in those grim months after Pearl Harbor. Frustration—if not "Rage!"—could be worked out through films like *Wake Island*, where our boys fought valiantly in the face of ultimate defeat. Note graffiti-like copy to convey trial of those early war months.

←
Scorched Earth (1942)

Greater shocks were had from war documentaries than all of monsters loosed during the conflict (Frankenstein, Dracula, and the Mummy enjoying quite a comeback), ads sparing no expletive to let patrons know that here was death enacted for real rather than Hollywood pretend. "Writhing wounded" and "mutilated civilians" were carrot toss to morbid interest of home-fronters who wanted to see war in ugliest terms.

←
Hitler—Dead or Alive (1942)

We'd take him either way in 1942, patronage likely wondering if *Hitler—Dead or Alive* might finish with the Führer's capture or kill-off. The ad promises sex as topping upon general depravity the Nazi chief embodied, and what better bargain for admission than Hitler being dealt with in such final terms?

↑

Hitler's Children (1943)

One of the biggest hits RKO ever had, but who remembers *Hitler's Children* today? Such ads as these probably told the story best. Women bullwhipped and sterilized was rawest meat to toss at wartime audiences, but blood was up for this sort of sensation, so came they did. Life under Nazi rule was topic of speculation for many a book and film, us imagining the worst and Hitler's crowd surpassing even that. What cut deeper, after all, than denial of sacred motherhood? War bonds and stamps would have done a brisk trade going out from *Hitler's Children*, if not coming in.

The gang that made Dillinger and Murder, Inc. look like "pikers" was Hitler and company, presented here as drug fiends, sex maniacs, or plain arch-murderers, each label being dream stuff of ads to sell this 1944 "Greatest Gangster Picture Ever Made!" Nazis as envisioned by wartime Hollywood were madmen one and all, wellsprings of perversion that movies before could barely hint at. Note free reference to Goering's morphine habit, Hitler as assassin of an underage girl (his niece!), plus rat-faced Goebbels, a most venal of vermin. Urgency to defeat the Axis trumped restraint earlier imposed on ads, rendering propaganda like *The Hitler Gang* an effective home-front weapon.

←

At Dawn We Die (1943

Sex was also the lure for you-are-there recount of "the rape of France," specifically fate of its "husbandless women" in lascivious grip of SS fiends. Ad liberties could be taken in such time of stress, so off came restraint where enemy misdeeds were shown.

←

March of Time: One Day of War (1943)

"Front Line Action Films from the Cameras of Dead Men" was stark selling for this March of Time subject hosted by Cincinnati's Telenews Theatre, the theatre issuing hearing aids so those impaired would not miss aural carnage that went with visuals. There was less limit on screen violence so long as based on combat reality, thus promise of "traitors executed" and "invaders cut to pieces" delivered on screen.

↑

Sahara (1943)

Leading men brought new credibility as action heroes in uniform. Here it's Humphrey Bogart just off *Casablanca* triumph as tank corps leader in Africa. Strongest ads put stars in valiant pose and armed to the teeth as first line of defense against enemy aggression. With men like Bogart in the fight, could any German force sustain?

→

Ravaged China (1943)

The Battle Cry of China (here retitled *Ravaged China*) was sufficiently unique and well made to stay relevant for the first several years of war, the documentary commending itself further for being in color. Produced in 1941, U.S.-shown from the following year, *The Battle Cry of China* was here a centerpiece at the Minneapolis Newsreel Theatre during December 1943. Newsreel houses saw a peak of popularity and attendance during WWII.

5th War Loan (1944)

War loans and stamps were a constant through the conflict, each theatre visit an occasion to be pressed for purchase at counters lobby-located between the box office and auditorium. There was no ducking expectant stares of bond sellers, nor fellow patrons who'd dug deep, "I gave at the office" a puny excuse for not buying each time you went to movies.

Where Are Your Children (1944)
Youth Runs Wild (1944)

Dad and big brothers being off to war left a junior home-front army at loose ends. Mom had hands full with ration stamps and not enough of staple needs, so who was to blame when youth ran wild? Ads reflected headlines and exploited rampaging teens, boys old enough for "lapping up liquor" and "petting" but not yet of age to don uniforms. Sex as usual was the sell, its being underage a boost to titillation.

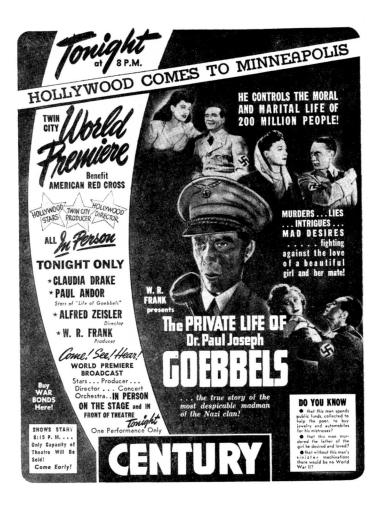

←

Invasion (1944)

By mid-'44, all ads needed was bold-lettered INVASION! to rouse interest in latest footage brought off European battlefields. Scoop-gathering newsreel theatres put footage on screens as soon as same was processed, each reel awaited breathlessly by civilians with stake in the fight, which by this time included everyone. Down-the-bill oldies *Scarface* and *Hell's Angels*, both dating from the early '30s, amounted to relaxation between latest headlines.

←

The Master Race (1944)

As confidence over war's outcome increased in late 1944, so did anxiety that "German highups, even in defeat," might rise again to befoul peace and possibly sire more "nameless babies." This last became a focal point for selling *The Master Race*, a warning that whatever the outcome on battlefields, there'd yet be threat to democracy. Ad makers found it hard letting go of scare themes even as the following year's victory beckoned.

→

Back to Bataan (1945)

Survivors from Bataan's death march lent
force to Chicago's first run of *Back to Bataan*, the title a reference to General MacAr-
thur's pledge, "I shall return," on occasion
of prior retreat. Now came going back and
getting even, John Wayne at the head of
retaliating forces. *Back to Bataan* opened
but months ahead of Japan's surrender and
several weeks after V-E Day, so crowds were
primed for final assault. This ad nicely conveys the squaring of accounts both on stage
and screen. A "command performance"
indeed.

→

Okinawa (1945)

Newsreel theatres by 1945 were the hottest ticket in
town, as here in Minneapolis, where a snow-bedecked
sig bids heat-waved patronage enter for freshest
glimpses of the decisive attack on Imperial forces at
Okinawa. Kamikaze footage was especially prized, its
shock value a reminder of resistance we still had to
overcome.

Post-War Jitters

The impact of the Bomb was too terrible for many to contemplate after the war, so films addressing the topic were sold by indirect, if not misleading ways, as here with the Cecil's sugarcoat for *The Beginning or the End*, MGM's account of atomic weaponry's development and wartime use. "4 Gallant Kids . . . in Love" was but incidental to far more serious content of the film, but who could blame ad artists for playing down fearful realities in favor of "fearless youngsters"?

When Celebrating Meant Moviegoing

f movie ads are any indication, the '40s must represent a peak of enthusiasm for holidays. Or maybe the biggest celebrations back then were confined to theatres. One thing's known: Holidays drew crowds like no ordinary period, there being natural impulse on the part of patronage to gather for festivities. Showmen kept charts of every known recess or jubilee, none too obscure to recognize for greater profit, theirs an ongoing wish that every day could be a holiday.

A Lady Takes a Chance (1943)

A Christmas wreath and tree baubles announce the Orpheum's holiday offering of *A Lady Takes a Chance*, an ideal gift for its combination of cowboys and comedy. Santa Claus was the surest bet to show up for Yule ads, a cheeriest and most expressive of year-end show promoters.

→

A Guy Named Joe (1943)

Endorsement by Easter Bunnies helped *A Guy Named Joe* gather eggs for the State's holiday weekend, the cartoon figures kept on file, reused annually, and often shared with neighbor town exhibitors in need of spring art.

←

Riding High (1943)

More cowboys with music and mirth, but this was what rang holiday bells in 1943, Santa assuring that "there'll always be a Christmas" where war bonds are gift-exchanged. These would be sold at the State's lobby-located victory counter, where much Xmas shopping took place at midpoint of the war.

←

Thanksgiving Shows (1944)

The Minnesota Amusement Co. had theatres all over Minneapolis, and so frequently ran combination ads featuring all member venues, the opportunity here to give thanks to patronage, employees, and Hollywood as source from which box-office blessings flowed. Turkey and pilgrim art were most familiar Thanksgiving ad devices, 1944's display seasoned by a 6th War Loan and opportunity to "play Taps for the Japs."

←

The Princess and the Pirate (1944)

Bob Hope and *The Princess and the Pirate* cast standing before Woods footlights in holiday attire was ideal means by which to hypo the comedy, now in a sixth week of Chicago play. Freshening the long-run show with Christmas-themed art often lured trade to an encore sit.

→

And Now Tomorrow (1945)

1945 wouldn't let Alan Ladd go in this New Year's holdover ad for *And Now Tomorrow*, in its third week and enhanced by fresh stage attractions to encourage repeat business. Cartoon impressions with big heads were oft-used and sure attention getters on Amusement Pages, especially where the "Hold It!" message was highlighted, as here.

→

The Bells of St. Mary's (1945–1946)

The Woods' first prediction for 1946: *The Bells of St. Mary's* will be "the happiest, heartiest hit of the year," a prediction borne out by the months it played that first-run engagement in Chicago. A New Year's baby with scissors and cutouts was handiwork of the Woods' always imaginative art staff.

Stage Spectaculars

The '40s meant a stronger embrace of live entertainment as an adjunct to films, mostly at urban venues, where theatres reaped benefits from swing music and bands at a summit of popularity. Ads could spotlight a big enough performing name and let the movies play as support. When Frank Sinatra or Glenn Miller were your acts on stage, who cared what was on the screen? If anything, pictures provided an opportunity for crowds to turn over or calm down after thrill-dose of the live star.

→

Martha Raye (1941)

Big-mouth Martha Raye sharing a bill with all-time screen classic *The Maltese Falcon*? Such odd pairings happened, and often, in '40s blend of oft disparate elements. What's best to remember here is that all entertainment and entertainers were but product to fill theatre time and hopefully turn profits. So which impression cut Chicago deeper—the Falcon's Mystery Jolt or Oh-Boy Martha's Cyclonic Fun?

↑
Glenn Miller (1941)

All-swing bills got the seat-filling job done, as here when Glenn Miller brought his Chesterfield Orchestra to the Palace and played live lead-in to swing-flavored melodrama that was *Blues in the Night*. The cigarette manufacturer was a radio sponsor for Miller.

↑
Frank Sinatra (1943)

Frank was at stardom's outset here but not yet dominating bills as he soon would, especially where an outstanding feature like *Five Graves to Cairo* shared the lineup. New York's Paramount Theatre often ran all night, sold war bonds, and herded screaming youth in/out of Sinatra shows as the singer's momentum built.

Comedy's Most Popular Team Comes to Columbus

Loew's Ohio landed a largest in-person catch of 1940 with Stan Laurel and Oliver Hardy, the Columbus venue being among stops along nation-wide touring for the beloved duo. Promotion and publicity made for a week of ads plus copy in local press, sampling of which is included here to illustrate the impact of major names on a populace upon whom stardust not so often fell.

We Invite 15 Journal Readers to See
Laurel and Hardy
IN PERSON
Plus—CLAUDETTE COLBERT and RAY MILLAND
In "ARISE MY LOVE"
Starts Friday LOEW'S OHIO
Scattered through The Journal want ads to-day are 15 names. Find your name and identify yourself at Journal office and you will receive a pair of tickets to Loew's Ohio.

←

Free tickets "scattered" through want ads assured that Ohio State Journal pages would get a close reading, plus fuel interest in Loew's Laurel and Hardy revue beginning that Friday.

↓

A first display ad announces the Friday bow of Laurel and Hardy and troupe of 30, children let in for just 15 cents.

↓

A Columbus Zoo visit and presentation of a gift monkey is promotion co-op between Loew's State and zookeepers, the Friday show date getting prominent mention.

LAUREL AND HARDY PONDER

NAME FOR MONKEY? THEY NOMINATE EACH OTHER

Stan Laurel and Oliver Hardy, famous screen comedy team due in Columbus Friday for a stage appearance at Loew's Ohio, are puzzled. They want a name for the perky little Garo ape, commonly known as a Japanese ape, which they will present to the Columbus Zoo. Laurel wants to call it Hardy and Hardy wants to call it Laurel. And that's where the matter now stands!

OLIVER HARDY, HUSKY, HAPPY AND HIPPY
Feature funsters frolic behind Ohio's footlights

"Babe" Hardy was caught by The Ohio State Journal cameraman in a special hello-Columbus smile as the bulbous comedian arrived with his partner, Stan "Weepy" Laurel, for a week's in-person engagement at Loew's Ohio. The Hardy mannerism of fiddling with his cravat is also in evidence.

This is the first visit of the famed comedy team to Columbus. The comedians are on a nation-wide tour, having arrived Friday morning from St. Louis. Their next stop will be in Pittsburgh, at the Stanley Theater.

←

Babe Hardy's signature tie twiddle merits news space in the Journal as he boosts an upcoming week of the team at Loew's State.

↓

The (Fri)day arrives, with shows beginning at 11:00 a.m. and continuing past midnight for the guest performers, Loew's State emphasizing ticket rates as "the biggest bargain ever to come to Columbus."

↑

Radio station WCOL broadcasts 15 minutes of Laurel and Hardy's stage revue live from the Loew's stage, sponsored by furniture seller Glick's, a well-known retail site in Columbus.

←

Tex Ritter (1944)

Western and hillbilly music had built plenty of momentum since the '30s, Southern houses especially receptive to backwood sound as here performed by cowboy star Tex Ritter and aggregation of pickers, comics, sidekicks, et al. The St. Charles in New Orleans had these plus local amateurs to be judged by Tex, an add-on to hypo local interest in the traveling jamboree.

↑
Ritz Brothers (1946)

This Chicago Theatre layout rocks the house to boost a second week "Roar On" for the Ritz Bros., a trio like the Marxes, but less known to generations succeeding them. Did the Ritz assault plus mirthquake of *The Bride Wore Boots* cause the building itself to double up with glee? The ad's strong suggestion they did was enough to draw crowds for an encore frame.

↖
Peter Lorre (1944)

The RKO Palace got all the big acts during wartime, mostly musical but sometimes such odd pairing as here with mystery man Peter Lorre sharing a bill with western sidekick Smiley Burnette, "Frog" in the Gene Autry series. The ad stresses Lorre's movie résumé and neatly stacks the four-unit program with emphasis spread among all.

↑
Belita (1946)

The Chicago Theatre converting its stage to an ice arena was major novelty for showgoers who thought they'd seen everything. "Spectacular" is the byword, Belita a proposed successor to previous decade's sensation, Sonja Henie. The ad announces a double serve of the skater, performing live and on screen in her latest Monogram vehicle, *Suspense*.

Spiced-Up Selling

Whether exploitation trash or mainstream product, ad makers doubled down on sex and/or mayhem where bills could use the boost. Films we would laud as classic received the adrenalin in case content was perceived too mild, thus lurid pitch on behalf of *The Magnificent Ambersons, My Darling Clementine*, and others. Movies were, after all, part of the same amusement wheel upon which burlesque and carnivals spun with their freak and kootch tents, so who cared about overlap so long as registers rang?

↑

The Birth of a Baby (1941)

Authorities had nixed showings of *The Birth of a Baby* in 1938, but Cincinnati theatres didn't give up. Three years later found the Telenews, normally a newsreel site, cleared for crowds who knew *Birth* would show just that, "before your very eyes." Whatever drama and chitchat surrounded the payoff didn't matter, so long as customers sat front row for a first-ever screen-shown miracle of life.

←

M (1943 revival)

A '30s German masterpiece, said many, but what did that matter to management at Cincinnati's Strand, where *M* was served like burnt meat for sex-seekers and students of twisted crime. Yes, the film was all about that (a child killer driven by sick compulsion), but who among *M*'s admirers could endorse its selling in such stark terms?

↑
The Magnificent Ambersons (1942)

Posters for *The Magnificent Ambersons* featured Norman Rockwell art, but selling realities obliged showmen down the line to salt ads with whatever sex the film's content implied, which in *Amberson*'s case was not much. Stopper words like *scandal*, *censor*, and *daringly* tried breathing box-office life into a show without the content to back them up.

↑
The Lash (1943)

Cleveland's Circle Theatre catered to base appetites, what with its reliance on horror films, sensational subjects, and sex bills like the one garishly promoted here. *The Lash* was actually *Lash of the Penitentes*, first released in 1936 and an exploitation mainstay for years afterward. *Pituri*, wherein a white woman is "stimulated" by native love potions, dated back as far but kept its odor at the Circle and like grind houses. What art the films lacked was at least compensated by an ad that deftly put lurid message across.

↑
Futurewoman (1943)

There was odd emphasis during WWII on giantesses, in this case 6' 7 1/8" Denise Darnell, who was sold on size and hopefully whatever dancing talent came with it. The Rialto cleverly hangs their barker off Denise's arm to emphasize Her Imperial "Highness."

↑
Super-Woman (1943)

Superman had lately come to movies in continuing cartoons, and here was his live-action counterpart at 6' 4". Lois De Fee is ad-presented as a challenge even to such efforts as measuring her. How could *Sherlock Holmes in Washington* as screen companion stack up to this?

↑ →

Tall in the Saddle (1944)

Sometimes even the apparent sure thing of a John Wayne western needed that little extra dose (of sex) to bait hooks. Chicago's RKO Palace uses the creative marketing of Ella Raines as Wayne's "pistol-packin' spitfire," and never mind the fact she never dons costumes like these for *Tall in the Saddle*.

↖ ←

Ecstasy (1942 and 1946)

Ecstasy was the specter from Hedy Lamarr's past that would not go away. It continued playing art and grind houses for as long as she was a star. Everyone from kids up knew that Hedy appeared naked in it, and who didn't want to see that? The film was a guaranteed house-filler through the '40s, ads such as these needing but to feature Lamarr and let a public's imagination supply the rest.

The Rialto Theatre in Chicago went to an all-girl policy during competitive wartime, a best of burlesque tempered by second-run movies and efforts to widen patronage beyond that sector normally found at strip houses and Burly-Q.

→

Sandra Sexton (1942)

Exotic dancers were often billed as the somebody-or-other of tomorrow, in this case "Girl in the Moon" Sandra Sexton as successor to Ginger Rogers, who'd also begun her career as an oft under-clad dancer.

←

Tirza (1942)

Burlesque star Tirza danced beneath a shower of champagne, an act presumably not duplicated elsewhere, or else why would the Rialto's ad feature her so prominently?

←

Dolores Lee (1942)

A direct appeal for "ladies" to "make him take you to the Rialto tonight." But what would ladies want with Dolores Lee and her Bumper Bunch? Only box-office receipts at evening's end would tell.

→

Mei Ling (1945)

Maybe it was outreach to our Chinese allies that brought Mei Ling to U.S. shores and the Rialto's stage. Anyway, the possibly Dali-inspired ad put eyes to staring at the "Chunking Cutie" as she displays celebrated charms to screen accompaniment of *Rockin' in the Rockies*.

↓ ↘ →
My Darling Clementine (1946)

Nothing was sacred in selling, not even a
John Ford western that would someday be
called classic. These ads for the Garrick
Theatre's first run of *My Darling Clementine*
are weighted with sex as primary theme, and
never mind that hell-cat and siren Linda
Darnell isn't Clementine in the film as ads
suggest. Darnell in heated posing was all
Garrick artists could summon to fire up an
austere retelling of the Wyatt Earp legend.

Selling Prestige

A classy enough attraction, preferably one based on a classic novel, could enrich as well as entertain, or so assured ads like this one for *Pride and Prejudice* (1940), which emphasized both book and Broadway hit origins. Contemporary slant is supplied by a modern couple's whisper of the theme, "how pretty girls teased men into marriage."

Novelist endorsement of a screen adaptation was cleverly used by the Roxy for Broadway's premiere of *The Razor's Edge*, a 1946 public eager to see how the screen would interpret the popular Somerset Maugham novel. Simplicity is keynote here for conveying class, with white space a best companion to dignified promotion.

"Adjusted" Ads

S howmen were notably timid where it came to period or costume product, figuring their public always wanted modern-set entertainment. "Please do not send any more pictures where they write with feathers," wrote one exhibitor to a distributor. Among quick-fix, if misleading, solutions, was to re-dress an ad to imply up-to-the-minute backdrop. Did audiences complain? If the movie pleased, we can assume they didn't; but otherwise . . .

→

The Devil and Daniel Webster (1941)

Deviltry down on the farm, but art suggests a cast drawn from fashion magazines, Simone Simon and Anne Shirley (the latter a beaten-down farm wife) looking not at all like this in the film itself, which was originally titled *All That Money Can Buy*. Showmen got one look and knew their public's money wouldn't buy tickets to such an awkwardly named show. Better to come straight to the point and call it *The Devil and Daniel Webster*.

→
Gentleman Jim (1942)

Period pics were a sweat for ad artists. They didn't trust costumes to translate into box office. *Gentleman Jim* is acknowledged in copy as the story of boxer James J. Corbett, a Gay '90s figure, but with period punch pulled via modern coat-tie-mustache art of Errol Flynn (he's clean-shaved in the film), along with upswept-styled and '40s-chic Alexis Smith as his romantic vis-à-vis.

→
Johnny Come Lately (1943)

James Cagney came off *Yankee Doodle Dandy* a bigger star than ever, went independent with *Johnny Come Lately*, and gave fans a new and gentler Jimmy. So, who needed that? asked showmen, who virtually to a man sold the film in most misleading action-and-free-for-all terms. Did customers complain? They certainly should have.

↑
Christmas Holiday (1944)

RKO Palace art staff misleads readers for the good of grosses in this happy ad for *Christmas Holiday*, the film itself a departure and downer for star Deanna Durbin, whose "greatest love-affair" this distinctly was not. If her vehicles wouldn't conform to Deanna's fan-preferred image, at least showmen could make promotion do so.

↑
Devotion (1946)

"Strange loves" among apparent moderns, so who'd figure this to be about the Bronte sisters from a century past? *Devotion* looks from this ad to be sister vs. sister with both in latest fashion, or did Emily Bronte prefer such décolletage as Ida Lupino displays here? Art of Olivia de Havilland looks borrowed from previous *In This Our Life*.

→
Kitty (1945)

Two theatres playing a same game with *Kitty*, a period costumer (18th century England) that exhibitors and their ad divisions dressed in modern raiment.

Chillers for Children?

Monsters that walked during the '30s fairly leaped the following decade. A process that would take them less seriously was under way by the war, and it seemed all of a sudden that horror had been given over to kids. Chillers were being packaged in pairs and given out with spook shows onstage that were lots more explicit than what screens could show. "All in fun" was watchword of spine-tinglers sold in terms of scaring the "yell" out of us.

$\rightarrow$

You'll Find Out (1940)

Here was one to get a new decade off to cheeky start; let monster masters Boris Karloff, Bela Lugosi, and Peter Lorre (the latter a bit more uneasily set among ghouls) spoof it up with "Old Professor" Kay Kyser and pave way to horror served light. Kyser in ad caricature was almost a creepy match for the terror trio, him forgotten today except by serious diggers into retro swing.

Horror Island and Man Made Monster (1941)

When spookers last but an hour each, it's best to serve by twos, thus "Double-Scare" of *Horror Island* and *Man Made Monster*, neither packing the gear to play alone but rich in imagery to decorate a busy ad like the Grand's.

Bela Lugosi in Person (1941)

Youth could laugh at Bela Lugosi's "Super Shock & Shudder Show" with its trussed-up "Virgin Maiden" and "Tarzan Gorilla" lumbering on-off stage, but the Lugosi name still had currency. Chicago's Oriental Theatre borrowed art from long-ago *White Zombie* (1932) to convey Bela's hypnotic appeal.

Stress on Shorts

All-cartoon programs were an ideal Saturday or schools-out ticket. Children mostly made up attendance, and as they were known treat-mongers, the concession area was assured of brisk sales. Ad artists, in both these examples, fell down somewhat on rendering Bugs and cartoon pals, the likeness recognizable if not altogether accurate.

Late as the '40s (and beyond), you could fill a kid show or art house with Charlie Chaplin enthusiasts. He was shorthand for funny even in shorts made a generation before. The Tramp pose and laughing faces herald this "brand new feature" culled from half a dozen of Chaplin's Mutual output, all dating from 1916–17.

↑

The Corpse Vanishes and Mad Monster (1942)

Sometimes ads got frisky beyond any chiller's capacity to deliver, art in this instance promising a prostrate nude whipped in her bed by a non-specific menace. This was taking liberty that sometimes got a theatre in hot water with parents and news editors.

Less Remembered Now Than
Celebrated Then

The Kay Kyser mention a few pages back was but the tip on iceberg of product and personalities that clicked huge in the '40s but are barely known today beyond celebrants of Old Hollywood. This was entertainment locked tight into the decade when it was new. Ads boasting Abbott and Costello, *Going My Way*, or star-spangled musicals of the day could go proud, strong receipts assured before printing ink was dry.

→ ↘

Keep 'Em Flying (1941) and Little Giant (1946)

Bud Abbott and Lou Costello were a huge novelty that got huger laughs, at least for a heyday that carried them through WWII as America's most popular fun-makers. The RKO Palace ad for *Keep 'Em Flying* wisely evokes previous hits *Buck Privates* (army) and *In the Navy* to pledge more of military-set mirth. By 1946 the RKO Orpheum could forego art and copy altogether to merely announce Abbott and Costello back in their newest, *Little Giant.* Such offbeat promotion would be risked only on surest things, and A&C at their '40s peak were clearly that.

←

Mrs. Miniver (1942)

Votes were unanimous: *Mrs. Miniver* was the greatest picture ever made—at least it seemed so in 1942. Radio City Music Hall had taken a poll that put *Miniver* at the top of all-time lists (note *Citizen Kane* at the bottom), this not news to millions who'd heard what a can't-miss this was. By the time Loew's Ohio in Cleveland had its booking, sellouts were virtually assured.

Going My Way (1944)

←↑

A clever gag customized by Century Theatre art staff for a Minneapolis ad showed well-known local park statue "Ole Bull" leaving his Loring Park stand to go and see *Going My Way* in its seventh week, the Century's gag being that even monuments can't resist the year's biggest attraction. A following week's ad sequel had Hiawatha and Minnehaha abandoning their park post as well (they'd been there since early in the century) to see the "heap good movie again." These promotions were trade-recognized as among cleverest of the season.

→

Someone could write a book about what a smash *Going My Way* was, much more a favorite than *Casablanca*, but that was distinctly then—times and tastes having changed much since. *Going My Way* stayed seemingly forever everywhere it played, urban markets seeing seasons change with it. Chicago called the Crosby charger a "road to happiness," that being truth for both audiences and enriched showmen.

←

A boast even Chicago could seldom make was one million people having seen a single film, but *Going My Way* did just that by its eighth week. Freshened stage shows helped as the run continued, Harry Richman a headliner for week four, then The Ink Spots and Lou Breese brought in for week eight.

Radio Revels

The radio-movie alliance may have peaked during the '30s but had energy yet for a coming decade, as evidenced by Fibber McGee and Molly, plus Bergen and McCarthy, all of them fairly twisted with eagerness to jump from microphone to large screens in *Look Who's Laughing* (1941). Caricatures tip off the fun cast, some of whom were familiar to film viewers, others less so. Interest was great in either case.

The Blue Network was an NBC radio arm, linked on this occasion with Chicago's RKO Palace for a stage/screen airwave salute at which listeners could see as well as hear their home favorites. So as to give clear signal, the ad for *On Stage Everybody* (1945) displays a broadcast microphone (twice) plus dancing imagery to hypo the live acts. Best of both worlds was thus cashed in on.

→

The Jolson Story (1946)

Al Jolson was old hat by the mid-'40s, so who would have dreamed his life story would become such a smash movie? "Word-of-mouth magic" was acknowledged as basis for 170,000 lining up over the first six weeks, an approving woman's eye casting a spotlight upon performing Jolson's image. A stunning 22nd week found radio's Phil Harris rewarding the 500,000th patron to *The Jolson Story*, an event newsworthy in itself. Lucky Mrs. O'Leary was but one of the enormous Jolson following that crossed generational lines and led to a 1949 sequel.

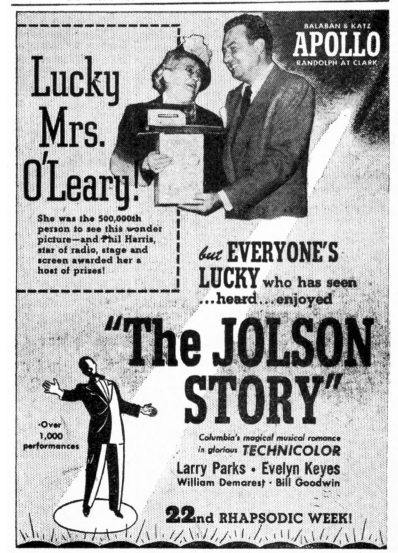

Sex for Art's Sake

The rise of art theatres after World War II was less because of quality European imports than earthy sex depicted in those imports, a sort of spice that censor-burdened U.S. features could not duplicate. Films from Italy were for a while most popular, each boasting street sense that Hollywood fantasy lacked. Ads for the arties were low-hung vines offering forbidden fruit.

→

Open City (1946)

Open City came with initial wave from a Europe just done with war, playing more like captured footage than narrative. "Plain sexiness" was accurate and what ads pushed hardest, but there were also rave notices from respected outlets to help patronage feel less like voyeurs.

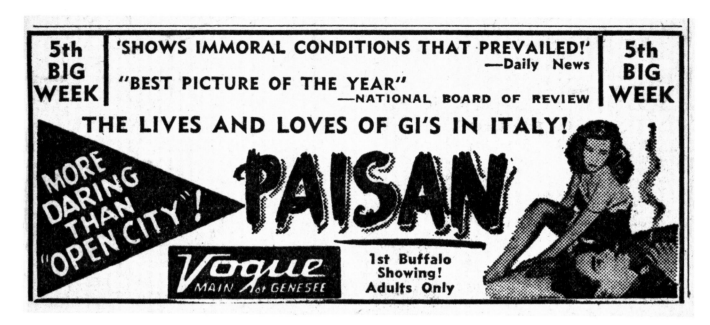

↑
Paisan (U.S. Release 1948)

Buffalo's Vogue Theatre played on wide suspicion that G.I.'s in Europe frequented prostitutes, contributing to "immoral conditions that prevailed." Comparison with *Open City* was apt, *Paisan* amounting to second helping of hot pasta to test local censorship and patience of newspapers running Vogue Theatre ads.

Paying to Greet the Enemy

Showmen imagined for a while that they could adapt television to their own ends, using it as another paying attraction for theatre customers. The concept was viable before TV penetrated a majority of homes and gave viewership the free alternative that spelled doom to many a movie house.

A '40s precursor to sports bars might have been programs like the Alhambra's screen offering of *D.O.A.* (1949), where patrons enjoyed big-screen baseball and wrestling broadcast in addition to the picture. Which was primary lure? Folks could by then watch b'ball or grappling for free in bars and be served alcoholic beverages besides. What ads couldn't mention was the dim picture cast by "life size" TV projection, a major reason the concept came a cropper for theatres.

Far fewer people owned televisions in 1949 than would be case just a few years later, so some theatres pitched regular programming as bonus entertainment at no extra charge. For the evening show of *Johnny Stool Pigeon* (1949) at least, this could take the place of short subjects the Alhambra would normally show.

→ ↘

Bitter Rice (1949–1950)

Were lady rice harvesters so compelling a topic, or was it fact they wore so few clothes when harvesting rice? This was sold on sultry strength of "full-bodied and gracefully muscular" Silvana Mangano, who awakened lust in Walter Winchell and critics from Bosley Crowther (*New York Times*) on down. Imports by now were less art than undisguised melodrama but still "committed to a type of realism not tolerated in Hollywood."

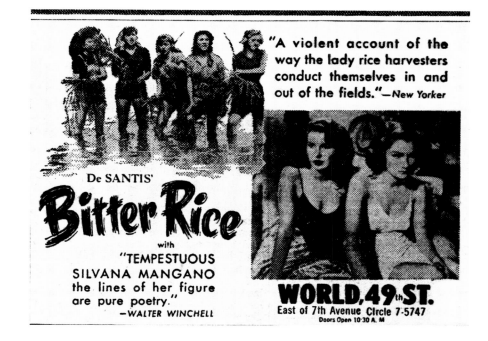

Making It Personal

Most if not all movies ran throughout the U.S., if not the world. It was up to ads to make each a local concern and personal necessity for hometown customers. That meant finding common ground between the show and audiences to whom it would play. Ads did this by linking shows with ongoing life within the community. A hit would be something everyone *must* see, or see again. Some locals became part of advertising by signing endorsements for a film or films they liked. You didn't have to be on a theatre's staff to participate in promotion, a showman's door always open to satisfied patrons willing to spread the word in print.

→

Love Crazy (1941)

The cartoonier the art, the clearer an ad's message that this is comedy. Loew's Stillman makes a second week of whimsy irresistible by minimizing star images, William Powell and Myrna Loy being long-established fun-makers, to favor Cleveland laugh response at *Love Crazy*. This was the sort of confident ad run by theatres where word of mouth was already good.

Babes on Broadway (1941–1942)

It took two Chicago loop palaces to ring in 1942 with the latest Mickey Rooney-Judy Garland musical, ads reflecting conviction that *Babes on Broadway* will fill seats at both. Here was a sort of attraction—*Babes*' nearly two hours of "Songs! Scenes! Laughter! and Heartbreak Too!"—that didn't need stage or live-band augmentation.

MADISON'S PREMIERE SHOWING!

YOUR OWN ARMY IN ITS OWN GREAT SHOW!

Brought to the Screen by
WARNER BROS.
For the Benefit of the
Army Emergency Relief Fund

Today get set for the most wonderful entertainment yet!

IRVING BERLIN'S

This is the Army

with Colors Flying in TECHNICOLOR

Produced at
WARNER BROS. Studios
FOR BENEFIT OF
ARMY EMERGENCY RELIEF FUND

STARRING MEN OF THE ARMED FORCES and
GEORGE MURPHY • JOAN LESLIE • Lt. RONALD REAGAN
GEORGE TOBIAS • ALAN HALE • CHARLES BUTTERWORTH and KATE SMITH
Directed by MICHAEL CURTIZ   Screen Play by Casey Robinson and Capt. Claude Binyon · Based on the Stage
Show Irving Berlin's "This is the Army" · Music and Lyrics by Irving Berlin
Produced by JACK L WARNER and HAL B. WALLIS

Thurs., Nov. 11 -- Armistice Day
One Performance at 8:30 P.M.
Admission: $5.50, $2.20 and $1.10
(Plus State Tax)

BUY YOUR TICKETS NOW!

TICKETS ON SALE AT STATE THEATER AND
REXALL STORE

(Only Capacity of the State Theater Will Be Sold)

ENTIRE PROCEEDS GO TO THE ARMY EMERGENCY RELIEF FUND

This message in behalf of the Army Emergency Relief Fund is made possible through the patriotic support of the Madison Business and Professional War Advertising program. Watch for Honor Roll appearing in later issue.

Hello, Frisco, Hello (1943)

San Francisco's legendary Fox Theatre makes it personal with this World Premiere splash for 20th Century Fox's musical *Hello, Frisco, Hello*, crossing off "Frisco" to proper-spell the host city. Local landmarks as film-featured and Fox stars in attendance swell this ad to must-see proportion.

Shadow of a Doubt (1943)

The newspaper headline gag is used to good effect in support of Hitchcock's *Shadow of a Doubt*. Center placement of "powerful hands" tips off strangling content of the thriller and lets readers know this is strong meat. Maybe the RKO Palace needed *How's About It?* with the Andrews Sisters for a calming co-feature.

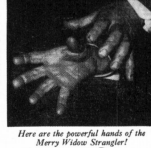

This Is the Army (1943)

WWI Armistice Day was still celebrated into the next war, and so was the ideal occasion for Madison, Wisconsin's State Theatre to open *This Is the Army*, a flag-draped musical whose receipts were donated to the Army's Emergency Relief Fund.

Pin Up Girl (1944)

Minneapolis pins up Betty Grable as its own *Pin Up Girl* in a clever bid to confirm her as the town's favorite. "Unanimous vote" eases the Fox musical into its second wartime week at the Century, 1944 a zenith year for escapist and Grable-graced entertainment.

→

I'll Be Seeing You (1944)

The Roosevelt chef serves up faces known and liked by Chicago patronage during wartime, all on spice shakers that earned trade plaudits for ad ingenuity, or maybe art staff was making the best of product that lacked a hook on which to hang promotion. For the record, *I'll Be Seeing You* was wartime romance between a shell-shocked sergeant and a female convict on parole.

→

Belle of the Yukon (1944)

A not-so-starry cast is loaded for bear as *Belle of the Yukon* gallops into Chicago, star heads laid upon cartoon bodies and copy pledging "gals, gold, and gaiety," along with "newest hit songs" by radio and platter favorite Dinah Shore. *Belle* fell into the something-for-everyone category typical of product offered during '40s boom years.

For Milady's Comfort

Folks generally lived more comfortably in theatres than at home. "Personal dream boudoirs" were the stuff of fantasy, like movies themselves. Ads boasting a newly installed rest facility were bound to seize notice, opportunity to experience such luxury a greater lure than even Van Johnson in *Easy to Wed* (1946).

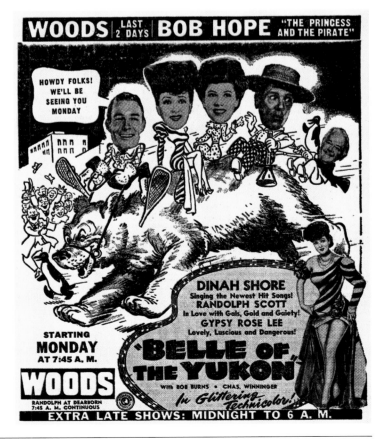

Thrill of a Romance (1945)

A motif frequently used in advertising featured stars entering theatre doors. Here it's Van Johnson playing on a phrase to describe swim-attired Esther Williams taking her customary dive. Customers followed suit (specifically Esther's), making *Thrill of a Romance* an enormous wartime moneymaker.

Johnny Angel (1945)

A frequently used ad gag had a holdover show blocking entrance to a newcomer, or in this case, the newcomer expelling a holdover. *Wonder Man* had been held over . . . and over . . . at the Chicago Woods, so it was for George Raft to kick out Danny Kaye and begin a hopefully as-long run for *Johnny Angel*. In flush days of 1945–46, neither was likely to fail.

↓
The Killers 1946)

What do you do with a show likely to draw men but not their dates? Arrange a booster to represent women "from all walks of life and vocations," in this case a Chicago housewife and an elderly one at that. If she'd go for *The Killers*, who wouldn't? Hardly a wonder that this one would play for over a month.

↓
To Each His Own (1946)

"No Children, Please!" increased cachet for parents. Would *To Each His Own* deliver on promise of adult entertainment? Praise from plain folks was always welcome when it could be got, but a show had to be truly special, like *To Each His Own*, for them to step up with name, address (!), and endorsement. Here was Balaban and Katz putting money where word of mouth was.

→

Gilda (1946)

Gilda was, in short, a sensation thanks to star Rita Hayworth and smoldering musical numbers you'd have expected censors to stop. Equal to this excitement was 4/20/46 reopening of the New RKO Pan, formerly the Pantages, which had begun as a vaudeville house in 1916 and led Minneapolis' show community since (it is still there and operating as a live theatre). Luxurious appointments and flowers for the first 100 ladies was but part of festivities that served as focal point of New Pan ads.

→

Naked City (1948)

A stark and effective ad for New York's own *Naked City*, the pavement-real police thriller shot on streets outside of and down blocks from the hosting Capitol Theatre. It was indeed a show "on everyone's lips," producing Mark Hellinger having been a leading columnist over many years. Note the soon-to-be-white hot comic duo Dean Martin and Jerry Lewis at the bottom of accompanying live acts.

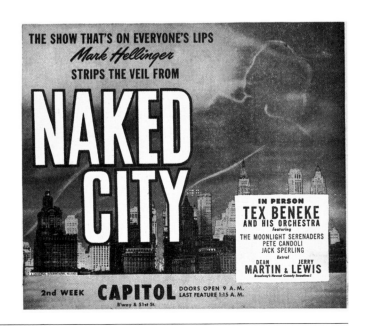

Still Giving Stuff Away

Dinnerware giveaway was mostly a Depression device for spiking attendance, but the '40s saw its application among theatres still in need of a boost. Trouble was, ads like this one could be mistaken for store promotion. Was it movies or dishes the Hollywood Theatre was peddling in this 1942 ad?

The best part of dating Judy in 1948 might have been the chance to win a "Universal Clean-Air Cleaner" or "Chest-A-Seat," whatever those two devices were. The Coronado had worked with Ellis Electric before on similar giveaways, preceded by guessing contests that would engage patrons for the week leading up, calling attention to both theatre and merchant.

↑

Rope of Sand (1949)

Ads could promote a career as well as movies, as here with Airline Glamour Girls, a Fox Theatre co-op with Trans-World Airlines that helped recruit women as air hostesses. The short may or may not have played beyond Minneapolis, where the stewardess school was located, but such a novelty, with a Trans-World agent in the lobby to encourage enrollment, helped hypo attendance to the Fox's feature offering, *Rope of Sand*.

↑

Holiday Affair (1949)

Here is a money-back-if-not-satisfied gag, and the patron must satisfy management that he/she honestly did not like *Holiday Affair* before admission is refunded. This was effective for ads— most customers figured a film had to be good to make such a reckless offer—but how many would demand cash back and bear the interrogation?

Of Course It Stays

Holdovers were a norm in larger markets where the '40s boom was most keenly (and profitably) felt. A "join the crowd" mentality made urgent the seeing of new and popular shows in first-run, which meant, of course, paying first-run ticket prices. Why wait and let excitement wear off?

→

They Met in Bombay (1941)

The cheering crowd with quotes was supposed to represent any night under the Loew's marquee during the first week of *They Met in Bombay*. Response like this had to merit a second frame, excited word of mouth taken for granted by the ad. You'd need a solid attraction to get away with boastful bally like this, which *They Met in Bombay* presumably was, even if not so well remembered today.

To Have and Have Not (1944)

Put on an "impassioned man-woman story," and you'd get your audience. Hot kissing, as in the urge, the verge, and the merge, was a tease to censors. You wonder if State Lake was first with the gag, because it's a dilly. A "hold on, baby" result was perhaps inevitable, as evidenced by full-length Lauren Bacall manhandled by Bogart just as in opening-day ads from four weeks prior.

Hellzapoppin' (1941)

A wraparound ribbon leading to the firecracker title puts Chicago on notice that zany *Hellzapoppin'* will have to go after a fourth and "positively final week," but who's to know if the RKO Palace will keep that promise? The design here is inspired, "Our mistake!" captivating the eye and directing it along length of the ribbon. Someone on staff deserved a raise for this job.

Since You Went Away (1944)

Ads would sometimes incorporate congratulatory messages to or from a film's producer or star, in this case David Selznick, whose *Since You Went Away* was a WWII home-front answer to *Gone With the Wind*. In this case, the Radio City Theatre thanks both Selznick and Minneapolis patronage for a success now in its third week. *SYWA* enjoyed similarly long runs everywhere during 1944.

The Dolly Sisters (1945)

A souvenir included with the Chicago Theatre's ad for *The Dolly Sisters*—images of Betty Grable and June Haver that could be removed and made into paper dolls. We can be grateful that the ad shown herein didn't get the scissor treatment, as many undoubtedly did by fans not necessarily confined to youth.

Price Points

Many a theatre ad appealed to bargain hunters, as here with the 1947 Atlanta Fox run of *Unconquered*, a DeMille spectacular that had played to advanced admissions elsewhere and was now down to popular-priced general release. As with *Gone With the Wind* and prior specials, ad copy emphasizes "not a spectacular second cut out," a legitimate concern as some longer features lost footage between roadshow and subsequent playdates.

Theatres were feeling the postwar pinch by 1948, enough so to lower pricing even on first-run Broadway, as here with the Paramount Theatre's open for *Saigon* at reduced rate. What with audiences diminishing and recreation sought elsewhere, the late '40s became a buyer's market for movies.

→

Along Came Jones (1945)

Blasting attendance records in Chicago was Gary Cooper in *Along Came Jones*, this ad more than misleading for the fact that there was precious little action to be had from this dullish western. The box office with hands held high was clever complement to the RKO Palace marquee indicating a second week.

→

The Kid from Brooklyn (1946)

Another view from out front—Chicago tourists hopping the guide bus to see Danny Kaye's latest uproar at the Woods. A cartoon lively as this, filling near entirety of an ad, could be plenty incentive for attending *The Kid from Brooklyn*. Not a few visitors to Chicago came specifically to see some of that city's grand theatres.

←

The Best Years of Our Lives (1946–47)

Like a magnet it drew them to the "most honored picture of our time," which *The Best Years of Our Lives* actually was, based on attendance records smashed and critic huzzahs. Academy Awards as an ad hook were used increasingly after the war, and since when had a picture won so many as this?

←

Duel in the Sun (1947)

Minneapolis gets *Duel in the Sun* for a hot, hot summer of 1947, during which the Selznick sex western played saturation in hundreds of venues throughout the country. Would 1,470 viewers lie in calling it "the most romantic love story they had ever seen"?

1950s

Wide, Wide Worlds

Selling the Spectacular

After harvest from a war came drought. Were movies less important to homecoming servicemen? Getting much of the eventual blame was television, and, yes, the free medium had it coming. Why pay for entertainment got for free and nearly as good? An ongoing baby boom made show-going a haul, and suburbs newly popular offered lots more recreation choices. Worse, whispers suggested that movies just weren't fun like they used to be, and maybe a more sophisticated public had grown out of them.

The industry reduced these conflicts to simple terms: Television was the opponent, and we must fight it. Combat was engaged in strictly Hollywood terms: Make movies bigger, if not better. TV couldn't be beat for convenience, but it could be dwarfed for size. New screen processes would be introduced, with excited ads there to greet them.

The immediate aim, then, was to spread the gospel of Cinerama, 3-D, and Cinemascope, plus numerous offshoots, and bring new excitement back to old fairground that was neighborhood theatres. Ads could but describe so much—how do you convey Cinerama within a few inches of page space? It was for ad designers to arouse curiosity, and this they did by promising things never seen or dreamed of on theatre screens.

This Is Cinerama (1952–53)

↑

The first '50s bid for all-encompassing screens was Cinerama, a 1952 arrival that tied up venues for years running and had to play roadshow to get back overhead increased by special projection. Crowds came thanks to Cinerama being a sensation that really delivered—yes, it did indeed "put you in the picture!"

↗

An assault on nerves was what Chicago's Eitel's Palace offered, much like riding a roller coaster like the one that opened *This Is Cinerama*. Engagements in a second or later year, as here, could tender Cinerama as a spectacle not requiring glasses as did rival process 3-D, which had come into vogue during the interim. Cinerama was imitated, but wouldn't be surpassed.

→

Cleveland sold *This Is Cinerama* in terms of exclusivity, as did most other hosts to the three-panel process. You'd drive hundreds of miles to duplicate this experience. An attractive woman squirming in her seat implied a host of possibilities and was ideal focal point for the Palace's ad. For such long runs, copy and graphics would have to be freshened to draw in not only holdouts, but repeat attendance.

→
Bwana Devil (1952)

A next revolution was distinctly down-market. Few dressed to come see 3-D as had been the case with Cinerama. *Bwana Devil* was the leadoff for a glasses-required experience of depth, Chicago selling the lowest denominator of lions leaping and women submitting. You'd only find out what a shill this was by showing up, letdown from which explains why 3-D was a short-lived fad.

↖←

House of Wax (1953)

Major studio expertise came not a moment too soon to rescue 3-D from quick-shot hucksters, *House of Wax* a first in April 1953 to really give patrons something for their money and strained eyes. Yes, it was still purest exploitation, but copywriters at least wouldn't embarrass themselves when referring to *House of Wax* in terms of "3-D as it should be seen—and heard."

3-D didn't work so well at drive-ins. In fact, it was usually an altogether bust. Maybe that's why Chicago's Original and World's Largest Drive-In (so they claimed) put near-equal emphasis on fight footage with Rocky Marciano and Jersey Joe Walcott. But wait; that was 3-D too. Must have been a trying week for outdoor patrons, what with shows starting at dusk, not a happy circumstance where setting sun met 3-D projection already dim at best.

↓

The selling language of 3-D came down largely to "firsts." There would be nothing warmed over about this novelty: Each offering had to provide something that previous ones did not, in Los Angeles premiere instance a first on the giant new wide-vision screen with amazing stereophonic sound. Obvious from the title was *It Came from Outer Space* being science fiction, but was *It* first for this genre in 3-D? So many more along similar line would arrive shortly to cloud our memories.

←

Another touted "first": 3-D music and comedy along with the depth feature, in this case an exhausting Chicago session with other-world creatures landed among Three Stooges nonsense. The ad stresses both, along with popular songster Nat King Cole—something for everyone, so long as they didn't mind donning specs for over two hours.

↘

It was a godsend when reviews were good for a 3-D, as critics tended generally to pan them, especially as the process wore out welcome. Press excerpts plus all those Clevelanders who "can't be wrong" was effective ad spin for a second week of *It Came from Outer Space*.

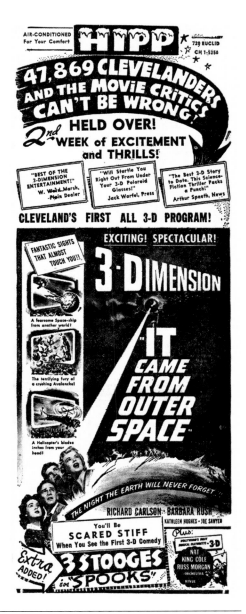

The Great Big Secret

This ad wouldn't reveal it, but 1952's *Above and Beyond* was about the atomic bomb and dropping of same near the end of WWII. Was this too grim a theme to promote outright? Better wisdom on the Oriental's behalf (Chicago) was to frame *Above and Beyond* in terms of mystery, as in a "billion-dollar secret," and hope that curiosity or the romance of Robert Taylor and Eleanor Parker would sell the show.

←

The Maze (1953)

Promising "new and perfected" 3-D glasses implied that the old ones had problems. By July 1953 and over half a year spent on the fad, even its adherents knew that depth could be shallow when specs went on fritz or projection kinked up. It became ad duty, then, to assure folks that this time, 3-D would work.

→

I, The Jury (1953)

Chicago was still drunk on 3-D as summer '53 brought thrill seekers out of the heat to see first *The Charge at Feather River*, and then a following week's *I, the Jury,* pre-sold not only by depth, but by hot author Mickey Spillane's sizzling rep. But what of poor Mickey Rooney, whose stage accompany gets barely a nod? The slipping star had to realize that times were sure enough changed.

→

Kiss Me Kate (1953)

3-D was on ropes by the end of 1953 and *Kiss Me Kate* arrival. MGM had, in fact, taken polls to see if showmen might prefer it flat. Most agreed to one more try at 3-D, so here was Kate in all her dimensions and that spanking scene besides. The ad posits *Kiss Me Kate* as the "first quality picture in 3-D," a rap on ones that had gone before, but not an altogether groundless claim. It was from the mighty Metro, after all.

Shane (1953)

There was an unseemly rush to widen screens during spring of 1953. Films produced in standard ratio, like *Shane*, were cropped at tops and bottoms so as to project across whole walls. So what if compositions were distorted so long as the image overwhelmed? Panoramas and stereo were what sold that year, and movies would have to adjust for them, at least until they could be filmed in accordance with wider expectation. Fortunately for showmen, *Shane* was a hit either way.

South Sea Woman (1953)

Question, then: Would a mirror screen be desirable, even if a "miracle" one? This was another attempt to revamp a standard-ratio feature into satisfaction of appetite for giant screens, the "panorama" a sudden must for theatres looking to ride ahead of curves. Note the fact that the Warner ad never specifically mentions a "wide" screen. Just square inches, as in 120,000! Correction to the copywriter, however, for such size wouldn't render a "brilliant picture," but rather a dimmer one, thanks to an image blown up so considerably.

When You Could Only Explain So Much

How would you have sold *Sunset Boulevard* in 1950 when it was brand new and no one knew what it was? Maybe a tip as to adult content or the Hollywood backdrop, as here for Chicago's first run at the Woods Theatre. Their follow-up excerpts a *TIME* review capsuling the story in a sentence, "faded movie star" and "kept man" a hopeful spur to attendance, but hardly revealing the greatness of *Sunset Boulevard*. Ads could do but so much—sometimes a public had to trust instincts and take a chance, as fortunates did for this eventual classic.

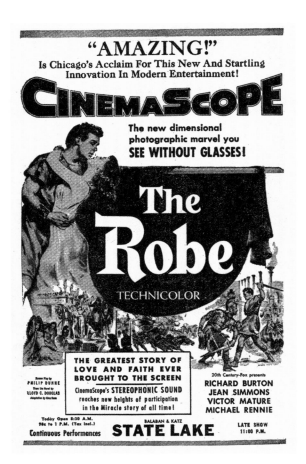

↑
The Robe (1953)

↑
How to Marry a Millionaire (1953)

Audiences were plenty sick of 3-D glasses, in fact of the process itself, by September 1953 when *The Robe* splashed down with its wider-than-ever Cinemascope, the modern miracle you'd enjoy without headgear. It was "dimensional," whatever that specifically meant. Maybe ads wanted us to know that *The Robe* had everything 3-D did, and then some. A big help was narrative content you'd not be embarrassed to bally, the Bible a surer bet for civic approval than lions hopping off the screen.

Cinemascope was a perfect gift for Santa to bring hungry exhibitors and novelty-seeking patrons. Christmas 1953 saw Claus huddled with sirens Marilyn Monroe, Betty Grable, and Lauren Bacall to tie *Millionaire* with yule-tiding 'round Chicago, ad art clear that Christmas just won't be Christmas unless we see "the big-time, grand-time, great-time show of all time."

Knights of the Round Table (1953)

Ads that duplicated the appearance of a Cinemascope screen were a given in early months for the process. This was the Hollywood premiere for *Knights of the Round Table* at the fabled Egyptian Theatre, site of starry opening night attendance. Listing luminaries was surest means of turning out thousands in the street to watch them arrive. The MGM Concert Hall as bonus implies a live performance, but *The Merry Wives of Windsor* was actually a Cinemascope short tendered as *Knights* companion.

↑

Cinemascope Rules Los Angeles (1953)

By the end of 1953, Cinemascope was a settled phenomenon, strong shows and weak making the box-office grade. This co-op ad for Los Angeles first runs reflects the grip Cinemascope had on the town and viewing populace. Between newest *Beneath the 12-Mile Reef*, continuing sensation *Millionaire*, and passing-torch *The Robe,* this was truly a 20th Fox-dominated marketplace. The ad effectively spells Cinemascope in largest vertical, rather than the customary horizontal terms used to trumpet the process.

The Black Shield of Falworth (1954)

Details to note in this Chicago ad: *Black Shield* star Tony Curtis leading a parade down State Street with radio's popular Irv Kupcinet as commentator. But wait; it'll cost 50 cents to park your car for festivities plus the show, and that's in addition to ticket price at the Grand. Is it a wonder folks drifted away from the movie habit?

White Christmas (1954)

Chicago's was a key engagement, so naturally they got *White Christmas* for 1954's holiday season. Farther-flung theatres weren't so lucky, many waiting until late winter or even spring '55 to see what new screen curiosity VistaVision was all about. The State Lake's ad, with its turkey meal imagery and horn of plenty, was effective inducement for folks to head for the show soon as Thanksgiving dishes were cleared.

Ring of Fear (1954)

That leaping tiger seemed like an old friend from 3-D days, but this was mid-1954 with Cinemascope now in the lead among screen novelties. Reflection of that is this Chicago ad wherein the wide process is unfurled three times, each in that distinctive style suggesting an engulfing image. Question remained: Could even Cinemascope make a movie star of Mickey Spillane?

←
Strategic Air Command (1955)

Quick now, what in heck is a curvilinear screen, other than another exotic label to entice a numbed-by-novelty public, and lost to proper definition since (at least by me). That plus all-engulfing depiction of a VistaVision screen was this ad's best chance at luring patronage to *Strategic Air Command*, another Paramount dig at primacy of Cinemascope.

→ ↘
Oklahoma! (1955)

Was that TODD-AO screen as tall as an elephant's eye, or ear, or whatever? Anyway, it was another miracle process, this one an admitted most spectacular of all, though by latter half of 1955, it was no longer enough to give them mere monster screens. There had to be something worth watching on them, as here with *Oklahoma!*, its must-see a carryover from Broadway. Here are two ads celebrating the musical's seventh month in Los Angeles, both with emphasis on TODD-AO as definitive screen swallower.

↑
Around the World in 80 Days (1956)

"Over and over again" was sweet music for any box office, repeat viewing a hoped-for outcome of playing roadshows for months on end. If *Around the World in 80 Days* stunned you once, why not come back and be stunned anew? TODD-AO is, this time, less emphasized than the mail order form for reserved tickets, plus respective pricing for favored seats and show times.

Be Casual in Your Car

Drive-ins were around well before World War II, faced slowdown in construction during that conflict, then came roaring back when service folk returned and births began booming. What better circumstance to watch movies than home with the family, "home" in this case a sedan-full of parents, kids, maybe a dog or cat—all in for single admission at many drive-ins, where food of restaurant (or at least grill) variety was also available. There were playgrounds beneath better outdoor screens, sometimes train rides, providing overall safe grounds for youngsters. A household could do every-thing here but hang wash (some sites did offer laundry service).

Ads for "ozoners" promised the moon, sometimes literally in cases where lunar imagery highlighted the peace and calm of amusement amidst clear sky. So much could be promoted beyond films being shown—a canteen with pizza, steak sandwiches, ice cream—so much of what "hardtop" concessions wouldn't offer for fear of spoiling seats and carpet. Ads trumpeted lots for little, as in all-night shows with donuts at dawn, features and fun for kiddies in such abundance as to make drive-ins seem like trans-planted circus grounds. Small wonder that outdoor theatres led the attendance field, often in refurbished fields, from the late '40s till gas shortage and changed driving/ recreation habits lowered the curtain on this show-going dreamscape.

ROSALIND RUSSELL & FRED MacMURRAY
"TAKE A LETTER DARLING"
SHOWS 8:30 & 10:30 P. M. MIDNITE SHOW ON SAT.

WORLD'S LARGEST **DRIVE-IN** WAUKEGAN & GOLF RDS.
STARTS TOMORROW—CHAS. BOYER IN "GASLIGHT"

↑

Take a Letter, Darling (1944)

Chicago's mammoth and "world's largest" drive-in opened on 6/12/41 to accommodate 1,160 cars over a 20-acre tract. There were "girl ushers on bicycles" that brought refreshments on request. You could even gas up your vehicle there and have tires checked. Full-moon imagery and a promise of "moonlit romance" conveys aura drive-ins had that hardtops couldn't duplicate.

↑

The Spotlight Is On (1951)

Locally newsworthy each spring were drive-ins gearing up for another show season, co-op ads like this pushing extras offered by participants. It meant lots to patronage not to have to dress up, park vehicles in town (in this case Cleveland), or pay sitters to watch kids. Here you could bring the menagerie along and tend them yourself, and maybe see (at least part of) a movie in the bargain.

←

Drive-Ins Are for Multi-Tasking

If the housework won't keep, bring it along. This couple, like so many others during boom years of outdoor show-going, make a drive-in seem like home.

When Charlie Was Toxic

Charlie Chaplin took a beating for "morals and politics" that would see him shut out of the U.S. by the time *Limelight* reached theatres in 1952. Showmen had to reject the film or sell it gingerly. The Woods in Chicago tried a cautious approach, as if endorsing the actor/comedian might get them in trouble, which in 1952 was distinct possibility. Los Angeles theatres meanwhile passed on *Limelight*, figuring why invite trouble?

←

Sugarfoot (1951)

Saddle up, Cleveland, for a Randolph Scott show-season opener. Westerns were a surest draw to outdoor theatres, and what more persuasive than "battlin' buckaroo" Scott riding head-on at readers? Night stars against black sky with cars arriving signal a crowded lot for the (well-named) Northfield Star Drive-In.

Calamity Jane (1954)

Toledo's Telegraph Drive-In had a monumental neon "T" on the back of its screen, seen by motorists for miles. When this place was open for business you knew it, as was also the case for the Parkside (aka the "Sundance Kid"). The skull for chillers and cartoon faces for lighter fare help balance the bills for this busy ad, focal point of which is Doris Day wielding her whip for principal attraction *Calamity Jane*.

Bugs Bunny Welcomes You (1954)

Cartoon characters were often used in drive-in ads to cue family benefits of attending. No coincidence then that Bugs Bunny and animated friends got heaviest play on outdoor screens. The 41 Twin in Franklin, Wisconsin, wisely photographed its "giant 130-foot screen" and used that as backdrop to award-winner features on tap, its ad artist adding Bugs as greeter.

The MM Gold Rush

Marilyn Monroe striking big led to grab for whatever footage could be had of her, even, as here in 1954, comparative oldies in which she had supported rather than starred. *We're Not Married* and *Let's Make It Legal* saw Monroe on margins, but fans wanted this star however they could get her. Loew's Esquire had but to center Marilyn on its ad and let ticket buyers do the rest.

↑
Country Music Holiday (1958)

Winston-Salem, North Carolina, loved that mountain rhythm, so it was very much a local event when the popular Flamingo Drive-In got a 1958 first run of *Country Music Holiday* as part of a three-hour hillbilly jamboree where it wasn't even necessary to mention the supporting feature by title. So long as it sang, it would sell. Getting there early for space wasn't puffery—these fiddle face-offs sometimes lined cars for miles down the highway.

←

Spotlight 88 (1958)

Don't know what life was like generally in Beaver Falls, Pennsylvania, but natives sure had fun at their Spotlight 88 Drive-In, what with dusk-to-dawn films, Funland train rides, and free Casey Jones caps for kiddies. It's anyone's guess how those "gigantic aerial bombs" might figure into 4th of July celebration.

↓

Spotlight 88 (1959)

Another barrage of entertainment for Beaver Falls. If anything, the ad suffers from too much of good things. Run-up to Labor Day 1959 (a new show every night!) would have exhausted the most stalwart drive-in goers, but who'd forfeit the chance to win that motor boat? Here was instance where an ad simply had more than it could effectively sell.

Holy Toledo—What a Show Town!

Toledo, Ohio, had a drive-in called the Miracle Mile. Its screen was 120-feet wide with a lot that eventually held 1,870 cars. Also, there was a cafeteria and extensive playground. Live entertainment was often tendered in addition to screen shows. The place opened on November 26, 1954 and from a start celebrated Cinemascope and all of biggest screen potential. A family could come here or go to Disneyland, and it wouldn't make much difference. Ads for the Miracle Mile were probably the best in the drive-in business. Trade magazines certainly thought so; they featured the Miracle Mile and staff often. What follows are but samples of inspired advertising for this outdoor entertainment legend, which was torn down in the late '80s and replaced by a shopping center. Progress, or poetic justice, has since closed the latter as well.

↑

Miss Sadie Thompson (1955)

Toledo could get cold, so bonus of a car heater with three features was meaningful to Miracle Mile guests. Cost of the warmers was initially a dime, increased later to a quarter.

→

Friday the 13th (1958)

Friday the 13th was always a lucky night for drive-in patrons, at least those that liked the scary stuff. Uneasily sat ads that used stock art for chills when running the mainstream likes of *The Buccaneer,* but the Miracle Mile ad compensates in part by adding *Terror from the Year 5000* to the bill.

↗

The Blackboard Jungle (1955)

With such fun on stage and at the Fantasy Playland, you'd think *The Blackboard Jungle* was mere afterthought, but Mom and Dad had to be enticed too, thus the "too hot" art to pump schoolroom savagery on view in the feature.

Bell Ringer (1955–1956)

Fireworks set off amidst crisp air for New Year's 1956 (and those heaters-heaters-heaters again) is capped by comped coffee and donuts with coming of dawn. The ad's bell ringer motif works nicely to tee off a whopping five features on view and all for a single dollar admission with kids in free.

↑
Satellite in the Sky (1956)

Here was Miracle Mile's answer to the Russians beating us in outer space—a satellite spree plus kitchen utensil giveaway for Mom. MM copywriters pledge a reveal of "the world's most guarded secret," but was that shared coming into or going out of the Miracle Mile's crowded lot?

↓
The Sock-Shock Shows (1958)

The Miracle Mile, like most drive-ins, was all about big numbers, as in 3, 4, or 5 features on a given night. Flavors were as often mixed for dusk-to-dawning, thus science-fiction abutting a western and a crime thriller—and, lest we forget, the Kolor Kartoon Karnival; a loaded plate, as was Miracle Mile policy, but ad makers must have realized that customers came mostly for on-site amusement other than movies.

Saturation Ads

A trend that began in the '40s and gained ground through the '50s was saturation, this being the opening of films at multiple venues or over multiple territories. Saturation would ultimately become a nationwide policy. Now it envelops the world.

Ads that promoted for packs tended to be large, with costs shared and participating houses mentioned in small print along with their locations. New York would cover whole boroughs for an opening, Los Angeles a wider expanse made up of hardtops and drive-ins. Exclusive runs were becoming more old-fashioned as the '50s progressed and folks demanded easier access to new movies.

↑
Love in the Afternoon (1957)

Between four participating showmen, you'd think one could have submitted a better ad than this. Clinging to Gary Cooper cowboy image sells short his departure into sophisticated comedy for *Love in the Afternoon*, but ad makers were often loath to stray from the conventional path of star promotion.

↑
La Parisienne (1957)

Sharing of costs between theatres allowed for vivid display of import sensation Brigitte Bardot, her name and image a shorthand for the advantage Euro films had over a still censor-hobbled U.S. marketplace.

←
Toy Tiger and The Rawhide Years (1956)

Los Angeles typically launched new releases in pairs and at far-flung sites. Downtown, Hollywood, plus smaller outposts hosted *Toy Tiger* and *The Rawhide Years* under roof; otherwise, it was a blanket of stars over patronage for this 1956 "explosion of fun and adventure." The ad nicely halves emphasis between the two, catering to both appetites.

Challenges to Censorship

The Production Code remained in effect through the '50s, and it applied to advertising as well as films. Rules often had been bent, but never broken outright without firm penalty. A restless public wanted better reason to abandon their televisions and other amusement for theatres, however, and expressed at box offices a desire for more adult content. Films would have to deliver upon promises made by ads. The era of bait and switch in promotion was fast headed for an end.

Tearing Lids Off

Sin towns were a scourge upon '50s America, said slick magazines picking scab off vice that infested towns small and large across the country. Embrace by films was inevitable, advertising spun off, it seemed, on smut tabloids that found illicit sex under all and sundry rocks. *The Phenix City Story* was based on ugly truth as told in *LIFE*, *LOOK*, and elsewhere, but then so was *Portland Expose*, ads for which boasted same investigative pedigree. "Family" periodicals, like family movies, were taking on looser definition.

← →

People Will Talk (1951)

Unwed motherhood was no laughing matter in 1951, but *People Will Talk* was intended as at least serio-comedy, its theme a spice rack for ads venturing toward propriety's edge. Note Chicago walk-back here: The Woods Theatre's initial ad lets Dr. Cary Grant tell single Jeanne Crain that she's "pregnant," while in a follow-up several days later, their dialogue is amended to words less explicit. Had Woods staff gotten a call to back off?

↑
Cocaine (1951)

Drug scare shows were a hangover from decades past. Soon enough there would be serious treatment of the theme, but till then came features dating back to the '30s, even if disguised as new.

↑
The Bad Seed (1956)

Search this ad for tip-off that *The Bad Seed* concerns a child who commits murder. Pretty much none to be seen, and yet word spread of taboo content thanks to the play from which the movie was derived, curiosity ripe as to how boldly Hollywood would confront it. These two Washington, D.C., theatres aren't taking a chance; they'll let readers find out someplace else what really happens in *The Bad Seed*.

→

The French Line (1954)

Jane Russell's ad bark had always been worse than her screen bite. Charlotte's Center Theatre spends space on Bad vs. Good aspect of *The French Line*, only bad to the theatre's mind being possibility of empty seats. Management was on defensive here: Had civic authorities tried to block *The French Line*?

Targeting the Teenagers

With recreation choices so splintered, theatres would inevitably give up on the family audience. If teenagers were loyal customers, why not aim ads directly at them? This was accomplished all too well, for now it seemed movies were excluding all but the adolescent army whose taste was questionable based on lowly exploitation they were fed.

Adults decried the junk heaped upon youth. Hollywood no longer sought to depict Andy Hardy values, but rather those of delinquent dragsters and girls gone wrong. Add to that monsters and rock 'n' roll and idols (like Elvis) that invited disapproval, and, well—there's your splintered market.

→

Mad at the World (1955)

Juvenile delinquency was a social issue made for movies, the nastier the better. Were there really "schools for murder"? A lot of grown-ups thought so. The Lyric's arrow directs us to a violent scene and leaves little doubt that it's a harsh show we'll chance seeing. You wonder how teens felt for being represented like this.

There's a New Best Actor in Town

Loew's Valentine in Toledo was like many theatres for seeing awards as stimulus to box office, basing promotion for 1954's *Suddenly!* on Best Supporting Actor nod that Frank Sinatra received for *From Here to Eternity*, a previous year's blockbuster that everyone knew and talked about. Novelty of the "song-and-dance man" turning loose "dramatic powers" would be ad emphasis for otherwise modest crime thriller that was *Suddenly!*

←

Giant (1956)

Far as teens figured it, there was one reason to see *Giant*, and that reason was James Dean. The Chicago Theatre got the memo and put Dean front-center in all advertising, contractual billings be hanged. They knew who built excitement and weren't for missing admission dollars spent on Dean since the youth idol died in a September 1955 car crash.

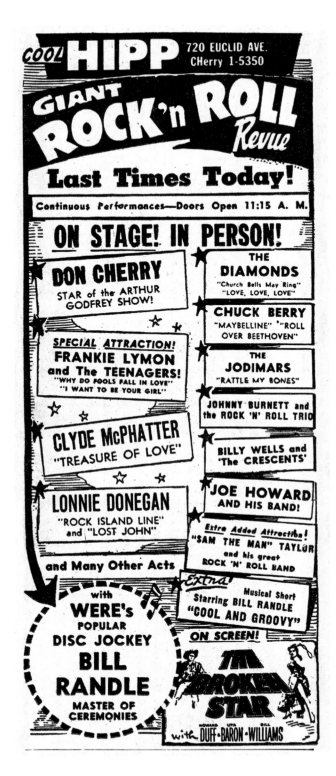

↑
Hula Hoop (1956)

How much could it cost to let teens bring their own hula hoops and supply stage entertainment for peers? The hoop was among the sillier of '50s fads, although few evoke as much nostalgia today. Who knew theatres could build a day's program around them and draw an audience just to see hula hooping demonstrated? At least performer youth got a rest while screen feature *Glory* was being unspooled.

Short Cut to Hell (1957)

→

A lot of parents felt this title bespoke a road movies were headed down, if not debased culture itself. For Miami Beach ad makers, *Short Cut to Hell* was shortest hand for what teens bought with loose change, honestly or otherwise come by. Civic authority saw such ads as instigators of youth disorder. Were they right?

Rock 'n' Roll Revue (1957)

←

Nothing stank for grown-ups like rock 'n' roll, full nights of it a dose of brain damage to malleable youth. The old stage band revues were never so extreme as this—11 acts!—with more promised. *The Broken Star* as feature offering was so negligible as to barely merit mention. The Cleveland Hippodrome had but to list performing names and let jockster Bill Randle lure in kids via his daily radio program.

Elvis (1959)

→

This ad gets no points for artistry, but who needed it when your attraction was R&R "King" Elvis Presley? He was cruelly taken from us during this period by military draft, so features he'd done earlier were played and re-played into guitar picks, fans oblivious to having seen *Jailhouse Rock* and *Love Me Tender* ad nauseam. They'd not forget Elvis, that was for sure.

Rick's Here with Some Other Guys

Like James Dean before him, Ricky Nelson sucked up all of ad oxygen when he made his movie debut with 1959's *Rio Bravo*, theatres such as the Paramount knowing that it was TV's teen sensation that youth would come to see. As to mere support that was John Wayne and Dean Martin, let the grown-ups sort them out. Management counted on Ricky to make box-office gardens grow.

↑
All Night Rock Show (1959)

Sometimes all you needed to fill a drive-in lot was essentially the same movie screened all night, in this case four "rockin' rolloramas" from known panderer to teens American-International Pictures. Surely attention wasn't on these, what with concession treats and what went on, or came off, in back seats. This ad would certainly set the mood.

And Still They Crept and Crawled

Horror films had long established permanence, and now came science fiction to join them. What with youth buying the most tickets, it was these chillers that floated many mortgages across the U.S. exhibition landscape. Spook stuff was known too for bringing in concession sales, this a comfort to showmen for it being money they could keep as opposed to paying out as film rental.

Ad makers flexed imagination with these way-out subjects, and fell back as well on tried-and-true promotion that had been in repeated use since pictures were silent. At shows like these, it must have seemed as though moppets and teens were all that remained of a moviegoing public.

→

Scream Show (1956)

Most every traveling spook rally had its man in gorilla skin, his spot a quick run through auditoriums snatching at girls and being pelted by spent cups and popcorn boxes. Ads for such scream shows were deliberately silly and keyed to '50s teen appreciation for irony. They were well past fear of such foolishness.

↑
Forbidden Planet (1956)

Sometimes selling needed that little something extra that a tie-in could supply, in this case a free ticket to *Forbidden Planet* that came in boxes of Quaker Oats. This was a nationwide promotion that some local showmen didn't favor, as it cost admission revenue and offered them no choice as to participation.

→
Invasion of the Body Snatchers (1956)

Science fiction subtle in approach was often jazzed up for ads. Showmen knew thrill seekers wanted a monster, so where advertised films didn't feature one, it was simple enough to add necessary elements, as here for *Invasion of the Body Snatchers.* "The Un-Humans" as pictured were entirely the creation of Hipp management.

↑

The Most of Everything (1957)

Wichita's Pawnee Drive-In puts "the most of everything" into a shiver-shake (and scream) ad placing horror/sci-fi with its natural cousin, rock 'n' roll. Knowing management may have realized by now that the "lost" adult audience lamented by trades was well and truly lost, ads such as here reflecting exhibition's surrender to new realities.

A Wonderful World of Color Selling

News printing was improved by the '50s, but color ads were still a rare indulgence and could be justified only where circuits had the dollars and enough member venues to justify the outlay. In this instance from 1955, multiple theatres in Milwaukee, Wisconsin, share benefit of Fox Theatres' splurge, theirs the only color display in an otherwise black-and-white Amusement Section.

→

The Curse of Frankenstein (1957)

A wedding of new with very old, this drive-in bill saw fresh-out-of-England *The Curse of Frankenstein* and its co-feature *X—the Unknown* backed up by ancient mariner *King Kong*, a relic made before most of his fresh audience was born. Still, *Kong* had cachet, and advertising would not ignore him.

←

It—The Terror from Beyond Space (1958)

Gimmicks to promote sci-fi were as limitless as the galaxy itself. The "free flight to outer space" involved enough caveats to make winning impossible, and you wonder if even kindergarteners for a moment took it seriously. We're still waiting, by the way, for the first "authorized, regularly scheduled flight" into space.

←

The Mummy (1959)

Give the Granada in Bluefield, West Virginia, points for creativity, being one of few theatres in 1959 that looked back to the ill-fated 1920s Carter expedition to sell a color remake of *The Mummy*. Ad usage of vintage news snippets implies a chiller based on truth, the fact it wasn't not apparent until tickets were bought.

↑

The Dick Bennick Show (1960)

WTOB was a hottest spot on Winston-Salem, North Carolina, radio dials, Dick Bennick their lead on-air personality. He also did spook rallies and rock 'n' roll shows at surrounding theatres like the downtown Carolina. Dick's 1960 Parade of Monsters didn't have to mention a feature title. It was enough that Bennick be there with buzz saws spinning and the "Frankie Monster" brought to life.

Let Friends Fill You In

This ad's "most exciting view in town" as shared with the film's principals was effective way for selling *Rear Window*. By a second week of Princess Theatre play ad readers already knew by word of mouth that this was 1954's crown thriller. Understated promotion could work where awareness was already keen and hard sell wasn't necessary.

When Movies Were Surrendered to TV

Under the heading of joining an enemy that had beaten them, Hollywood forsook its theatre partners and began selling off back libraries to dreaded TV in 1955. They'd done it surreptitiously over several years before. The avalanche buried exhibition, hundreds of '40s and older movies tube-bound and free but for sitting through sponsor spots.

Broadcasters schooled themselves on the ad style theatres had used, an effective instrument now turned on the very men who'd perfected it. Worse was newspaper ownership of many stations, which meant they'd favor publicity for television. Ad art for the latter often ran beside theatre space on Amusement Pages, sharp eyes needed to tell which from what. Bargain hunters had but to ID the freebies and stay home for an evening's recreation, and why not, when print promotion for movies on TV was as compelling as that for theatres?

→

Jack Webb (1948/1954)

You could call this a surrender—anyway, it was sad. Once dominant picture houses now traded on the popularity of television stars to sell movies they'd done before home sets conferred immortality. Here it's Jack Webb, a bigger name in the '50s than most on marquees, supplying reason for folks to forsake TV this once to see him on the Lyric's large screen, never mind that both these features dated back to 1948.

←

Warner Bros. Movies on TV (1957)

Well, who'd turn this down? The best of Warner Bros. library, and running nightly (daytimes too) on Sacramento's Channel 3. Full-page newspaper ads like this were a first, but not final, thrust into theatres that could scarcely compete with films given away so freely. Is it a wonder that showmen felt studios had betrayed them?

←

The Early Show and Big Hit Movies (1958)

Comic strip ads like these seemed to mock theatres being shoved aside on Amusement Pages. Here are televised "first runs" for *Captain Scarlett,* a 1953 release, and *Flame of the Barbary Coast*, a lavish John Wayne less than 15 years old.

The African Queen (1951/1958)

Stunned was Los Angeles' viewing public when local channel KNXT premiered blockbuster *The African Queen* on Saturday, October 11, 1958, among first major post-'40s features to be telecast, this a soundest argument so far to stay at home for your movie entertainment. *The African Queen* was even broadcast in color for those few with sets to receive it. KNXT and sponsor White Front Stores laid a haymaker on struggling competition that was L.A. theatres.

From Free TV to Paying Screens

The old Our Gang comedies, renamed The Little Rascals, broke big on TV in 1955, kids so besotted that they'd even buy tickets to watch the shorts in theatres. Same was the case with *Trouble on the Trail*, merely a paste-up of Wild Bill Hickok episodes starring Guy Madison, that series a home hit since 1951. Maybe seeing such familiars in a crowd situation made the paying more palatable. Anyway, it was cheap babysitting offered at the Princess for New Year's Eve 1956.

The West Point Story (1950/1961)

If the '50s were bad, the '60s got worse when films of post-1948 vintage landed by the hundreds on the home screen. KHJ-TV in Los Angeles treated each like a premiere, as here with its 1961 broadcast of *The West Point Story,* presented by Household Finance Corp. Theatres no longer had an exclusive on movies as an event.

River of No Return (1954/1964)

KHJ's rival L.A. station KTLA fought back with the bigger gun that was Marilyn Monroe in *River of No Return*, while Channel 9 used *East of Eden* with James Dean as counterpunch. Local TV outlets waged movie ad wars of their own as theatres looked on helpless.

Almost Like Ringside

That new western in Technicolor (*Drums Across the River*) was less than a footnote to main event that was live boxing on the Cleveland Hippodrome's "giant theatre-size-screen television." Emphatic selling this was for a one-time 1954 event, theatres trying a level best to harness dread force that was TV.

←
Living It Up (1954/1966)

Networks got many of the best recent movies and drove stakes deeper into beleaguered box-office hearts. Dean and Jerry seem here to be celebrating business they'll take away from theatres when their 1954 comedy *Living It Up* plays to millions more in 1966 than saw it on a paying basis.

1960s

A Slow Slide Down

Rates Rise, Ads Shrink, and
TV Takes Over

To live through this decade was to watch movie ads drift toward inconsequence. That's a personal opinion, of course. Some might say movie marketing crested here, then improved steadily after. I suppose it comes down to which side of the '60s break commands your sentiment. One truth was this: Theatre ads in newspapers had become less important. Promotion relied on television to spread word of films on the way. Spots amidst network programming got notice in ways cold print never could, the more so as color viewing made headway through the decade.

Not to say newspaper ads disappeared. They'd remain plentiful; indeed they became more lavish as theatres twinned and installed luxury features, such as plush rocking seats—would sofas be next?

Let's call it an autumn decade, with effective ads falling like golden leaves upon ground not so green. Veteran managers and layout folk were still active and, provided they had the budget, could remind us that well-drawn ads served as a most effective tool in promotion's kit.

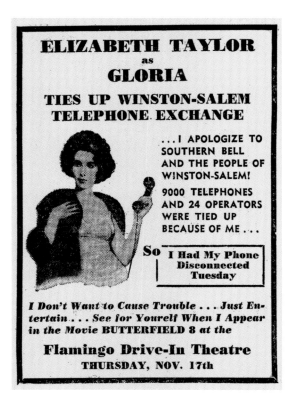

↑
Psycho (1960)

Fitting indeed to begin the decade with a thriller that jumped track of everyone's expectation and introduced a strict rule, actually enforced in 1960, that no one would be admitted once *Psycho* began. Alfred Hitchcock's image and direct address to readers was not unlike his weekly TV intro, everyone cued to the uneasy attraction set for premiere at New York's DeMille and Baronet Theatres.

←
Butterfield 8 (1960)

Did Elizabeth Taylor's *Butterfield 8* character really tie up all of Winston-Salem's telephone service? Flamingo Drive-In management wanted us to think so, then head for their lot to find out what the excitement was about. "Butterfield 8" of the title refers to call girl Liz's private number, so naturally ads ran with that phone "connection."

↑
Inherit the Wind (1960)

Carolina manager Dan Austell figured *Inherit the Wind* was a cinch to clinch Best Picture for 1960, so much so that he'd stake free tickets against a loss. Wonder how many Winston-Salem folks came back to collect after *The Apartment* took the award. No sweat for Austell—the gag surely swelled attendance for *Inherit the Wind*.

↑
The Grapes of Wrath and Tobacco Road (1960)

Heartland and Deep South cinemas held certain oldies in reverence, two at top of lists being 1940's *The Grapes of Wrath* and from the following year, *Tobacco Road* (updated here to "scorching . . . lusty . . . dynamite" effect). Rentals for both were cheap for being ancient and on TV besides, so go figure the Heart Drive-In in Kansas City, Missouri, filling its lot every time the pair came back, more recent *God's Little Acre* a little extra spice this time.

↑
Wild River (1960)

Down-home sellin' for pseudo-arty merchandise that was *Wild River*, a Fox flop made into a hillbilly hit by the State's selling staff. Muddy and fist-swinging imagery barely represent the film, this an obvious rush job of an ad for a tough show to sell.

→
The 57 Outdoor Drive-In (1960)

And still they drove in, the '60s a glorious last stand for under-stars watching. The 57 Outdoor Theater, located on the old state highway outside Grafton, Wisconsin, touted its "no squint" screen and food that was "mmm'm," with wise emphasis on kid amusement. It was small communities such as these that would be last to let go of the beloved ozoners.

↑
Day of the Triffids (1963)

Another Dan Austell creation shows a Triffid drawn beside Winston-Salem's landmark R.J. Reynolds building and invites us to compare size. Another case of local ingenuity brought to bear on a scare show that likely did better than expected after Austell turned his capable hand to it. The trade should have built a statue for this guy.

↑
It's a Mad, Mad, Mad, Mad World (1963)

Another star-studded Hollywood premiere, this time shared with opening gala for the Cinerama Dome, a legendary showplace still operational. "SOLD OUT!" was a phrase exhibitors liked using, it being prod for folks to not miss a next showing.

↑
Early Bird Matinee (1963)

An odd aspect of '60s moviegoing was early matinees "for the ladies." The Cinema Theatre in Greensboro, North Carolina, sought 580 of them (presumed seating capacity of the house) to share the "joyous treat" of free taxi service in, with free coffee and donuts for the extreme A.M. run (6:45!) of *Breakfast at Tiffany's*. Freebies resulted from tie-ins with local merchants. The Cinema would remain food-friendly, closing and eventually reopening as a pizza-and-movie house before doors closed for good in 1980.

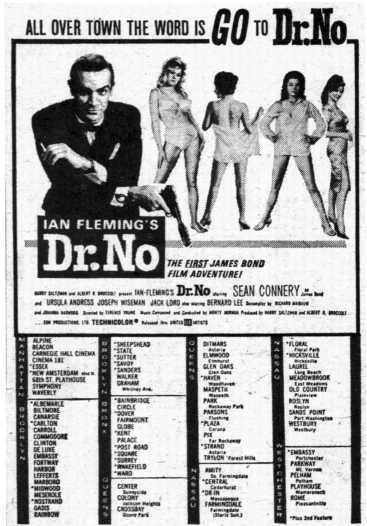

↑
Dr. No (1963)

"All over town"—New York City and environs, that is—"the word is Go to Dr. No," a good play on presumed word-of-mouth for the first James Bond adventure. Ads were customized to indicate a series before *Dr. No* was seen, this reflecting confidence from distributor United Artists and theatres alike in a phenomenon to come.

→

Mary, Mary (1963)

Charlotte's brand-new Cinema I and II, located at the city's first shopping mall, served as both summit and climax of grand theatre building for developers making a last stand against rival recreations. Color as utilized for this full-page ad was equal to grandness of the 1963 event, and yes, Cinema I and II remained the largest and most grandiose screens Charlotte had to offer for years to come—until ultimately torn down.

→

55 Days at Peking (1963)

Los Angeles goes all out with full-color promotion for another epic, this one more would-be than fully realized. The concept of exclusive engagements remained viable as of 1963, provided the picture lived up to promise as shouted in ads like this. Projection in 70mm was by now supplanting Cinerama as giant screen experience of choice.

↑
Doris Day-Dreams (1964)

Drive-ins often devoted nights to a popular star. Most commonly saluted during the '60s were John Wayne, Elvis, Jerry Lewis, and queen of the grass-and-dirt lots, Doris Day, whose backlog was dredged and put to service until changed times made her kind of comedies passé. The "Day Dreams" stock art could be used whenever the actress was featured, an oft-occurrence throughout the '60s.

↑
My Fair Lady (1964)

Movie tickets as a Christmas gift? In 1964 it made sense, certainly where the attraction was *My Fair Lady*, reserve ducats ordered by mail and at premium price. Hollywood's Egyptian Theatre ran this holiday ad shortly after Thanksgiving 1964, figuring to fill reserved seats throughout weeks before and after Christmas.

→

My Fair Lady (1964)

The Capri in Charlotte, North Carolina, retained sole custody of *My Fair Lady* for much of the Eastern Seaboard, in fact all the expanse between Washington and Atlanta. If you wanted to see the season's biggest musical, at least in 1964 or through most of 1965, you'd make the drive, or take the train for *My Fair Lady*'s Capri engagement. Many did.

→

The Killers and The Lively Set (1964)

Small town drive-ins were very much about "hot cars, hot thrills, and wild women," primal needs perhaps better met while viewing (and doing other things) in great outdoors. The Starlight was where cars (some surely hot as what was on film) convened in my hometown, this ad one I clipped from the local newspaper in 1964.

↑
A Hard Day's Night (1964)

Stampedes for *A Hard Day's Night* were very real for first runs of the Beatles debut. The Flamingo Drive-In in Winston-Salem, North Carolina, hooked a leviathan here and did turn-away business during summer weeks of 1964. Were downtown hardtops asleep? Traffic watch: Imagine how latecomer driver/passengers "raved and howled" when Flamingo staff hung "Full Up" signs each night.

MOVIE GOERS—Friday night's block long lineup for the opening of a new film at Rochester's Chateau Theater evidenced teen-age spending for entertainment. The attraction is "Thunderball." The film is the fourth in a series of Ian Fleming "James Bond" spy thrillers that are the current rage. (P-B Photos)

Thunderball (1965)

Newspapers that carried a theater's advertising, and were paid for doing so, would from time to time sweeten the arrangement by running news items related to a show. In this Rochester, New York, instance, it is a "block long lineup" along wintry streets waiting to see *Thunderball* at the Chateau Theatre, the same issue carrying as well a Chateau ad encouraging repeat attendance with, "If you've only seen it once, you haven't seen it at all."

↑

Harper (1966)

Credit Warner Bros. more than the DeKalb Theatre in Illinois for this trend-setting boost for *Harper*. Irony had seeped into ads by the mid-'60s, in deference to seen-it-all patrons who got this sort of mystery-detective stuff coming and going from current movies and television. What to do except mock such tired formulas?

←

Battle of the Bulge (1965)

Another from my scrapbook to reflect '60s fascination with luxury features at Charlotte show houses. The Village was shopping center-located, very much a trend at the time to connect to retail business. If *Battle of the Bulge* proved a disappointment, at least there were lounge chair seats and acres of free parking.

← Carolina Kiddie Show (1966)

Saturday or schools-out proved occasion for kid shows made up of low-rented product (mostly oldies) and a master of ceremonies, often as not a local radio or TV personality. Dancing on stage to music from a live band was permitted, in fact encouraged, and bingo saw prizes distributed among youth. Such programming would thrive through the '60s, become less common in the '70s, and fade fast by the '80s.

→ Wild in the Streets (1968)

Springfield, Massachusetts, ushered in a counterculture's era of ugly ads for uglier exploitation like *Wild in the Streets*, the line drawn clearer between films for protest-minded youth and entertainment adults would seek. But grown-ups were increasingly written off by showmen, because weren't they all by this time watching their TVs at home?

← The Graduate et al (1968)

Theatres through the '60s were jumping from singles, to twins, and beyond. Here at Springfield again was a go at a triple, the 1, 2, and 3 split between shows a public would turn out for (*The Graduate*), and ones they'd leave alone (*Half a Sixpence*). The ad artist does a neat job of juggling attractions for each of three screens.

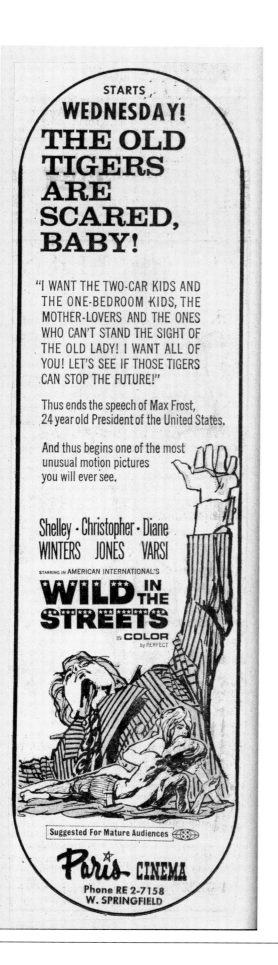

↑
The Wild Bunch (1969)

The Chicago Theatre confronts its public with a show they're challenged to forget, underlying message being that if you want pabulum like what's served on TV, then stay home and watch it. This between-eyes selling became necessary as exhibition faced another bleak season.

275

Afterword

here are still movie ads in newspapers. Plenty, in fact, just not so abundant as before. The difference is priority, which ads lack in current hierarchy of promotion. What was once a most vital means for spreading film word ranks near the least today. Not to sound last rites, however, as pages in many a Sunday section still herald what theaters offer (the *New York Times*, in this sense, like old times).

There's no denying greater sophistication in modern selling, as borne out by innovation online and in theater lobbies. Digitized movie posters have taken the place of rolled or folded ones, thus saving time, printing, shipping, and accumulation of spent paper. Progress has retired old ways just as it's discarded film itself (again by digital). To argue for a return to celluloid or heavy presence on Amusement Pages (what survives of them) would be like trading electric power for gaslight.

I won't argue that things are worse, lament Good Old Days, or seek to turn back clocks. Besides, the really good newspaper ads, like anything outstanding, were always in a minority. Were I more a tech maven, *The Art of Selling Movies* might plead as effectively for digital as dawning of a new epoch in showmanship.

In fact, I think we are better served by leaps taken so far in the 21st century, just as when talkies and eventually television opened frontiers of entertainment. What I've sought through *The Art of Selling Movies* is reader reflection on a singular means of promotion, and how it encouraged a prior century's immersion in movies. Theater advertising could be lurid, silly, plain foolish, and sometimes . . . lovely. For a gone era wherein they flourished, ads were a daily menu of mixed flavors, infinite variety, and pleasures enough to occupy seekers for a lifetime, even as samples herein barely scratch a surface of what's out there.

Index